Embattled Witness

Father Bernard Häring, poly-lingual author and lecturer, teaches moral theology at the Lateran University in Rome. He is best known for his work in medical ethics and his most recent book is *Ethics of Manipulation,* also published by The Seabury Press.

Bernard Häring

EMBATTLED WITNESS

MEMORIES
OF A TIME OF WAR

90
A Crossroad Book
THE SEABURY PRESS·NEW YORK

The Seabury Press
815 Second Avenue, New York, N.Y. 10017

LIBRARY OF CONGRESS CATALOGING IN
PUBLICATION DATA

Häring, Bernard, 1912–
Embattled witness.

"A Crossroad book."
1. Häring, Bernard, 1912–   2. World War,
1939–1945—Personal narratives, German. I. Title.
BX4705.H14A33   940.54'75'0924 [B]   76–13556
ISBN 0-8164-0312-0

Printed in the United States of America

v

ACKNOWLEDGEMENT

I heartily thank Mrs. Josephine Ryan who during the past few years has again and again urged me to write these wartime memories. Now she has patiently transcribed the tapes, and typed and edited the manuscript for this book.

Introduction

IN view of the many books that have been published about memories of the terrible years of the Second World War, the reader may ask why this author wants to tell his story.

My intention is not to add to the massive testimony about the horror and cruelty of the war, the crimes of Hitler and the suffering caused by war, although these should never be forgotten as warning against future wars and national policies that might lead to war. My chief reason for writing these recollections of my own experience is to show that, even in the midst of all the crime and inhumanity of the war, there was so much goodness in people on all sides.

This story, then, is first of all an acknowledgment of the enormous debt of gratitude which so many people of various nations have deserved. And while it is gratitude to them personally, it is also thanksgiving to God.

The reader may find here, too, a story of God's providence. I have sometimes said that I do not *believe* in divine providence, because I have come to *know* it. I have seen it and touched it.

For some who have followed my efforts to contribute to the renewal of Catholic moral theology, this story may also be enlightening as to the background and the kind of providence that prepared me to work to overcome a one-sided ethic of obedience and to teach instead a morality of personal responsibility and brotherly love, with courageous adherence to one's own sincere but ever-searching conscience.

Embattled Witness

[1]

The Gospel of Healing in Wartime

To provide a background for my recollections of various wartime experiences in France, Russia, and Poland, I must first convey a general picture of my service in the German army.

I was among the first Catholic priests who, in November of 1939, were called into the German army's medical service. I received an eight-week training course in Munich and was sent immediately to a division of infantry service. In January of 1940, however, my religious superior obtained, through a Catholic general in the medical corps, a temporary leave of absence for me so that I could teach in our seminary until September. It was during that time that I conceived and worked on the main outline of my book, *The Law of Christ,* which was finished in the years after the war.

The following September, I was called back to army service and given a second training in the medical school in Augsburg. From there I was sent, late in the year, to a division stationed in France, near Bayeux, Normandy. This was, for me, an especially fortunate assignment, since both the commander of the regiment and the doctor to whom I was assigned were practicing Catholics, and I could dare to celebrate the Eucharist and to preach every Sunday for the soldiers of my company. It must be understood that in the German army at that time it was absolutely illegal for priests who were medical aides—not chaplains—to engage in any pastoral care for soldiers or lay people, or to conduct any religious service.

Almost all the soldiers of my company attended the eucharistic celebration each Sunday, and a few capable men soon formed a good choir. Somewhat later another opportunity came, again on an unofficial basis, to arrange a regular Sunday mass for German soldiers in the cathedral of Bayeux, one of the most beautiful medieval cathedrals in France. Every Sunday I bicycled from our station in Somerville to Bayeux to celebrate mass and to preach the gospel. Eventually, our commander heard of this and put his own car at my disposal for the weekly trip.

One Sunday after mass, when I was still using the bicycle, the military commander of Bayeux stopped me on the street. I was startled and, of course, expected a severe challenge about my illegitimate action. But the opposite occurred. He greeted me in a friendly way and said, "I attended your mass and liked it. If you wish, I shall be glad to ask the military music corps to participate in it. I am sure they would welcome the opportunity." So each Sunday thereafter, we had a beautiful musical program, the fine old cathedral was almost filled with soldiers, and many French civilians also attended.

Because I knew some French, I acquired a rather privileged position in my company, which took me on various errands around the city; and since my time did not have to be strictly accounted for, I was able to build up some very good relationships with the local people. As a result, I could offer pastoral help, and sometimes medical help, to them and to our own soldiers.

Throughout the whole war I was to follow this pattern of friendship with the civilian residents in whatever towns or villages we were billeted. But in the days to come this would be a far more difficult and dangerous course than in this relatively quiet and decently governed spot in Normandy. For Germany's war with Russia, involving two dictatorships, alike in their lust for power and their determination to stamp out the religious spirit which so directly opposed their tyrannies, would soon begin.

Early in May of 1941, our division was transferred to Poland, the area around Sokol. Our company, composed entirely of medics, was stationed in a village that had no church. My soldier friends soon set up an altar in a huge empty barn. There we had mass for our company and for other soldiers stationed in the neighborhood. Civilians, too, began to attend as word spread that the Eucharist was being celebrated. Since it was the month of May, I also inaugurated services in honor of the Blessed Virgin, a popular devotion in Poland.

But the word had apparently been spread too carelessly, for soon I was called to task by the commander of the battalion. A malicious trial was arranged. My crime was not only that I had friendly relations with the Polish population but that I had even celebrated mass with them in spite of the Führer's law prohibiting such things.

Following the accusation, the commander, who was brusque but apparently fair, asked if I knew that I was acting against the law. I did not deny it. Finally he asked if I would like to say anything in my own defense. I answered that I could not defend myself, but only asked the favor of having my case treated with that of the second lieutenant who had accused me. (I was not supposed to know who had accused me, but a friend had told me.)

When I asked this favor, the second lieutenant, who had been standing there listening to the trial, stiffened and his face became very red. The colonel asked what case I referred to. I answered, "The case is that this man has surely been in much more intimate rapport with the Polish people than I. While my relations have been only on the basis of prayer with good, honest people, the lieutenant has been drinking and dancing with the kind of Polish girls with whom I do not associate." The commander then dismissed me with a few hard words and took up the case against my accuser.

It may be an open question whether my action was very Christian or not. However, with a sincere conscience I made it a practice throughout my service in the army to defend myself directly and to unmask the dishonesty of my accusers. I was convinced that those in power usually tend to use pressure against people who are timid or cowardly but would rather leave in peace those whom they cannot intimidate.

THE evening before the war with Russia began, we were all quite aware of its imminence. I was called by the official chaplain of the division and asked if I would hear the confessions of soldiers in one of the nearby churches of Eastern Catholics. A great many soldiers made their confessions that evening. On the way back to my company afterward, weary from so many hours in the confessional, I unexpectedly saw a young officer who had been my classmate in high school. He was loudly berating his soldiers in harsh and crude language. The sight so depressed me that

I crossed to the other side of the road so that I would not have to salute him. Did I thus follow the example of the priest and the Levite who did not want to meet the poor man who had been robbed and wounded? Here was one of the unpublicized horrors of war: the ugly "little Caesars" who abused the power they were given over other men.

This officer, who came from an excellent family, had been a gentle and generous fellow when I knew him in school; but like so many others, he had later been manipulated by the system that exercised a tremendous influence on those who wanted to make a career of the army. I met the man later in Russia when times were very bad, and realized that there was a noticeable conflict in his heart between the culture of his family and the style of the career officer.

On the way back to the barracks, I was accompanied by my best friend, Brother Fichter, a Jesuit student, a wonderfully good and gifted man. Knowing that the war against Soviet Russia would begin within a few hours, we talked very seriously about the prospects of the Church and the world. I expressed my dismay about the insane war and my readiness to give my life as a prayer that men might free themselves from the age-old slavery of hatred and war. I saw no bright future, I said, for people like us. My friend, on the contrary, insisted, "I do not want to lose my life in this senseless business; I want to spend it for something worthwhile. When the war is over, there will be a great task ahead of us, as ministers of the Church, to serve people and to work for a better, freer world."

Toward midnight, everyone knew that only a few hours remained before we would go into battle. I invited my friends to a prayer service. Crowds of soldiers, including officers of the whole regiment, assisted at the penance service, the general absolution, and the eucharistic celebration. No distinction was made between Catholics and Prot-

5

estants. I celebrated without altar and altarstone. It was one of the most moving experiences of my priestly life. Everyone knew what it meant to receive the assurance of peace with the Lord, and the body of Christ as a promise of everlasting life.

At the first sign of dawn, our company passed the boundary line and came under attack. And the first man who needed my help—as priest, for he was beyond medical help—was my dear friend and brother who had been so vitally alive only a few moments before, and so anxious to survive in order to rebuild a world gone mad. Brother Fichter had been struck by a shell. His head was shattered and his brains spilled out like water, even while his body was still alive and wrestling against death.

I was utterly overwhelmed, and cried bitterly. It was the first and the last time I wept during the war. Very soon things became so difficult that, if one were to survive, one could not give in to his feelings.

THE next man to whom I had to minister was a Russian soldier who was close to death. I did my best to clean and medicate his wounds and then tried, in both the Russian and Polish languages, to speak to him about the prospect of his last hour. He was, however, of *Circassian* origin, and could not understand what I was trying to say.

I showed him my little crucifix, hoping that the cross would indicate to him that I was a priest. He already understood that I was truly a friend, and accepted my help gratefully, but he did not understand what the cross meant. He asked, "What does that thing mean?"

In the midst of so much suffering, I was again saddened because I could not convey the last consoling message to a man who was a brother in Christ, one redeemed by the blood of Christ.

But the battle went on, and we had to move forward. I could not find time even to bury my friend. As never before, I felt my helplessness—but I also felt the meaning of being there to heal, to console, and to share that "peace which the world cannot give."

[2]

Medic and Priest
in Hitler's Army

MY wartime service as medical helper brought me to a deeper understanding of Christ as savior, as physician, as the one who comes not to judge but to heal.

There is a strong affinity between the priestly and the medical ministries. For me, despite army regulations to the contrary, the two became totally integrated on the battlefield, and scarcely less so in my relations with the local civilians in whatever areas the fates of war stationed us. Indeed, so complete was the merger that, in at least one instance, it caused a bit of humorous confusion. A soldier came and addressed me, "Herr Feldwebel [Sergeant], I want to confess my sins." I laughed and told him, "Well, I would not confess my sins to any sergeant." We agreed that he would confess to me, not as a member of the army or of any degree of officialdom, but only as a brother in Christ.

When the war with Russia broke out, I was still in a specialized company of the medical corps. During the first week, in response to our own offer to go wherever our help was most needed, three of my fellow priests and I were transferred to different regiments of infantry. Each battalion of about eight hundred men had a doctor and a trained medical helper, besides other medical aides. Frequently, in the absence of a doctor, the main responsibility for the health and often for the lives of these men fell upon me as medical helper.

The division to which I was assigned, and particularly my own regiment, was composed mostly of Catholics of the various Germanic tribes—Bavarians, Silesians, and so on. They quickly learned that, besides being available to them for medical service whenever they needed me, I would celebrate the Eucharist for them whenever possible, serve as confessor or spiritual adviser at any time, and would bring them, if it became necessary, the last anointing and the consoling message of Christ in the Eucharist.

On occasion I gave general absolution. This was allowed and encouraged by the Church during wartime, especially for those facing immediate danger. The condition for giving general absolution at that time was that we would explain that sins are truly forgiven for those who are repentant and of good intention, but that all who were convinced of having committed mortal sin would later have to confess individually when opportunity presented itself. During these war years, many who were surely not in the state of mortal sin came to individual confession, and many who received the general absolution after many years of absence came back later for individual confession.

Throughout the war I carried the Blessed Sacrament in a pyx in my pocket, and often when I told fatally wounded men that I could give them Holy Communion and the last anointing, their gratitude was so great that the misery of wounds and death was almost forgotten.

Perhaps the experience of a single day on the battlefield may best illustrate the actual opportunities to act as priest as well as medic in spite of prohibiting laws.

Our regiment, thrown into a fierce battle near Kharkov in October of 1941, was ordered during the night to attack a village occupied by greatly superior forces of the Russian army. We were driven back with heavy losses and had to dig ourselves into trenches outside the village. The man next to me, as we were digging in, was a fine Catholic fellow whose parents I had once met in our seminary. He had just returned from leave after being wounded. That night he was among those who lost their lives and to whom I gave the last rites.

By morning, the Russian tanks and troops were moving toward us with such tremendous power that more and more of our men began to run away. Finally I, too, ran with the last of them, and only my quick legs saved me. The Russian tanks followed at our heels until finally we were able to hide between the houses in the next village. The Russian artillery was already shelling the village, and as we crouched there, five soldiers from another unit were hit by a single shell. I went to help.

When I opened the first man's clothing, his bowels fell out. I covered him and told him gently that I was sorry that it was too late to help him medically but that I was a Catholic priest and would gladly offer my ministry if he wished. The man responded, "I am an Evangelical Christian, but if you have a word of comfort I will be grateful." I told him, "It is God, our Father, who now calls you home. Say 'Yes'." And in this terrible situation he answered, with great peace, "When God calls us we are always ready." I had to go then to help the other four badly wounded men.

That afternoon we were ordered to counterattack: a futile and costly effort. Under the fire of the Russian tanks and infantry, we had now lost at least half of our soldiers by death and casualties. There had been four medical helpers under me; now, all four were dead, and I was running from one place to another, from one wounded or dying man to another, in an open field where everything could be watched by the Russians.

Then, after digging ourselves in again, when I was finally in a foxhole, head down, utterly exhausted, I heard agonizing cries, *"Sanitäter!"*—the call for a medical aide. The cries came from a neighboring unit to which I did not belong and for which I had no military responsibility, and I decided that I had done all I could and would move no farther. But as the cries became more anguished, I knew I had to help. I ran and found the man, a huge, tall fellow from the southern Tyrol. I started to carry him back to the trenches but saw that his situation was hopeless. I told him then that I was a Catholic priest and had with me the Blessed Sacrament. At that, the man opened his eyes in astonishment. "Oh, how good God is to me!" he said. And he was all the more grateful because he apparently felt quite unworthy of such a grace.

In all such cases, I informed the parents, spouse, or relatives whenever I could about my last encounter with the man as he faced the hour of his death. In this case I sent the message to his parish and later received a letter from a priest who was his cousin, telling me about the man. A few years earlier, he had left the Church as a result of a sharp confrontation with the parish priest who was surely in the wrong. He very soon regretted his action but had not found the courage to return to the Church. However, he was known always to have been ready to help other people, especially lonely, elderly people. And now God had allowed me to bring him the last comfort, the great sign of peace. At that moment, I felt that to have brought this message to this good man made all the troubles and dangers I had gone through that day worthwhile.

For myself, it was a great school of life to carry with me the body of Christ, always in view of Christ's readiness to meet his friends, to meet everyone who wanted to prepare himself for a decisive hour.

I had a great advantage over the military chaplains because I was not in the ranks of officialdom. In my activities as medical aide, I met the men in their daily needs and could minister to them in either of my capacities, as priest or as medical helper.

ONCE, after a hard battle, I found a Russian soldier, who had been wounded several hours before, lying in the field. I took care of him as well as I could, and he, wanting to express his gratitude, offered me all the money he had. Poor man, I still remember how disturbed he was when he saw that I did not welcome his gesture. Perhaps I had been too abrupt or emphatic in my refusal. But soon he was able to understand that the greatest reward for me, in this criminal war, was to be able to help a man who was on the other side but whose faith and mine were in accord.

Always and everywhere, the Russians showed astonishing gratitude even for services which were not only necessary but which should have been taken for granted.

WE were in Kharkov from October until just before Christmas of 1941. Then suddenly we were loaded into lorries to be transported northward to a front where the Russian army had broken through and we had to fill the

13

gap. We were nearly frozen in the lorries and did not yet realize the extreme seriousness of the military situation.

In the lorry with me was a Catholic soldier, brother of two priests, who had expressed to me a few days earlier his deep regret that, because of illness, he had been unable to come to the Sunday mass; however, he hoped to be able to come on one of the following Sundays.

As soon as we were unloaded from the lorries, this young man joined me and said, "I want to make my confession right now. I have a feeling that I am close to my last hour." So while we walked, he made his confession with striking humility and trust. I still remember the sincerity and purity of this wonderful person.

A couple of days later, I heard from his friends that he had been killed while trying to save a wounded comrade.

STRONG bonds of friendship developed with the men I served. The medic, and even more the priest, who lives with and for his comrades finds appreciation and trust which encourages him in his service.

From almost the first week of the Russian war until I was wounded in May of 1942, I served in the same unit of an infantry battalion. I had hoped that after my recovery I would be reappointed to the same unit and could rejoin my friends, but I was appointed instead to a *Beobachtungs-Abteilung,* a specialized battalion for observing enemy positions and measuring the site and range of artillery.

In this new unit I was once more medic and priest in an inseparable synthesis. As new friendships developed, I wanted to stay with these men. Several times sickness or recurring wound trouble offered me the chance to be sent back for convalescence or reconvalescence, but I preferred to stay where I was. Once, during our second winter in Russia, this decision proved to be a bit foolhardy.

For a time, our battalion had been without a doctor. The commander suggested that I take the job since, by now, I had a good deal of experience and was in any case doing the work. But finally I contacted the surgeon general who made appointments, and he sent a doctor, a fine young man who, although knowledgeable, was only recently out of the university and therefore without much medical experience. We cooperated very well. In general, he accepted my advice in matters where I had more experience. On one occasion, however, he stuck to his own opinion, with rather grave consequences for me.

He brought to my room a soldier whom he thought had a minor ailment, and asked me to take care of him. After a close look at the man, I told the doctor that he had typhoid fever. Somehow the doctor could not bring himself to accept so quickly my correction of his diagnosis, and insisted that he was right.

By the next day the man could no longer be transported to the hospital, so I had him as roommate until the critical period was over. When I did bring him to the evacuation hospital, I noted that the doctor had still put his own wrong diagnosis on the accompanying document. I therefore suggested to the chief doctor that he examine the man carefully. A half hour later he returned and confirmed that the man had typhoid. "And now that you have lived with him," he said, "I invite you to stay here because you are surely contaminated."

Instead, I returned immediately to my unit where, two days later, I found that I was indeed contaminated. And

15

since it was already too late for me to be transported, I stayed in my room and took care of myself. But even when the critical point had passed and I could be moved, I stayed on. I was too much attached to my friends to risk reappointment to a different unit.

[3]

Priest and Medic
for Russian Civilians

WHEREVER we were stationed, my two ministries were as much combined in serving the civilian populations as in serving our soldiers and the Russian prisoners of war. If, for the soldiers, I was a medic who served also as priest; for the civilians, I was more a priest who served also as medic.

Normally my contact with the civilians would start with my good army friends bringing me wounded Russian soldiers and civilians. Wherever they saw great suffering, they told people that their medical helper was a priest and that he surely would try to help them. So work and opportunities to help were never lacking.

Ordinarily, this medical help for the civilians was on my own time and of my own volition, but during the late spring and early summer of 1943, when we were stationed in the Pripet Palude (swamp) area, it was also a military assignment. The whole area was infected at the time by various contagious diseases—typhoid fever, spotted fever, and others—and since this posed a serious threat to the German army personnel, the military decided to extend medical care to civilians as well as to the soldiers.

Since my orders were to serve wherever I was needed, I spent a great part of my time in the surrounding villages visiting the sick, giving medicines and prophylactic injections, and trying to improve the appalling hygienic conditions. I was rather strict about imposing hygienic measures. For instance, families with sick members had to use different wells from those used by families who were still untouched by fever.

The people were most appreciative. I still remember their coming from a distant village to my quarters when the strawberries ripened in June, to bring me the first fruits of the season, a touching sign of their gratitude.

Only in one village a slight difficulty arose. Some of the older people said, "The priest is very kind to us but he does not seem to be orthodox. He thinks that sickness comes from our wells and marshes and from the toilets; he doesn't believe that it is God who sends it." However, in a few friendly discussions, this problem was at least partially resolved.

B UT not all the troubles for which I was called were caused by contagious diseases; some were caused by contagious emotions. Like the fight I was called upon to stop one night after people had been drinking their *samochon,* or homemade whiskey.

A man had been accused of adultery, and members of his wife's family were beating him unmercifully. It was hardly the kind of duty I wanted, but by intervening and shouting orders above all the clamor of the brawl (God gave me a strong voice!), I managed to put an end to the fracas.

The next day both parties came to me to express their thanks for stopping them. They had come to their senses in the meantime, had seen the foolishness of their actions, and had been reconciled.

On another *samochon*-induced occasion, the man in whose house I was staying came home in incredible pain, as if his bowels were burning. Washing out his stomach gave him no relief; I needed oil. But nobody in the neighborhood had any oil. By now the poor fellow was loudly crying, *"Matka pomachai!"* (Mother, help me!) Finally it dawned on me that the resinous oil I had with me might have the same soothing effect as any good oil. I gave it to him and he soon fell asleep. Again, there were thanks in the morning.

Another case—whether *samochon*-induced or not I do not know—was much more serious. It happened on a day when both the doctor and my assistant were absent. I was therefore alone in my office when a terribly injured young man was brought in. In an argument, a fellow worker had driven a dungfork into his head. The wound was deep and long; his brain was uncovered.

The people who brought him in to me were in despair, and I not less, because I did not dream that I could help him without other assistance. The nearest civilian doctor was at least three hours away, and there was no hope of reaching him. Besides, the people said he would not come even if we reached him, because they were poor. So finally, seeing that nothing else could be done, I told the man's friends to leave me alone with him and I would do what I could.

After injecting a narcotic, I did a careful cleaning and then sutured the whole thing. (I already had considerable experience in suturing, since the doctor did not like this kind of delicate work and often had me do it.) I did not think that the man had much chance to live. However, at my disposal was the new antibiotic sulfonamide; I also gave him some vitamins and other medications.

To the surprise and gratitude of his people, as well as of the fellow who had wounded him—and surely of myself— the man recovered in about five weeks. The reconciliation of the two men gave me almost as much pleasure as the cure itself, since it meant that another deep wound had been healed.

ANOTHER of my experiences was, to say the least, unusual for a priest. Early one morning, while I was still saying my prayers after celebrating the Eucharist, a young girl rushed in, breathless, with the message, "Mother sent me. Please come right away because my sister will die if you do not help!"

I recognized the girl. Only a short time before, I had treated her sister's husband for typhoid fever; so now, thinking that his wife had caught the fever, I took my little kit and hurried with the girl to her home. When I arrived, I found the room filled with family members and neighbors, all huddled together in shared anxiety. And then I discovered, to my surprise and embarrassment, that the trouble was not at all typhoid fever; it was a case for a midwife!

My first reaction was one of impatience. I told the grandmother that she should know that I was a priest and that, while I could treat contagious diseases or wounds, I certainly had no qualifications for handling a case of childbirth. "You should call a midwife," I said. But she answered, "We don't have midwives; this is always the task of the *babushka,* the grandmother." "Well, then, *babushka,*" I said. "You must take care of it yourself."

But despairing voices were raised. They pleaded. The grandmother knelt before me. "You can help if only you want to, and you must help. She has been in labor for two days and two nights, and I have done everything I can. Now she is exhausted. She will die if you do not help."

I realized then that even if I did not know what to do, I had to do something, if only to show my good will and to give them some hope. A great murmur of relief went up when I reached for my kit, but I for one did not share in it. I was trying to decide what to do. Finally, I gave the young mother two injections, one of kardiazol to strengthen the heart and circulation, and another of caffeine, a strong stimulant. Then I left the room and went out to breathe some fresh air.

The *babushka* followed me outdoors and asked if things would now be all right. I said, "Let us pray that they may be all right." And soon we heard a call from the house for *babushka*. When I realized that things were developing well, I started to make my way home, but my little messenger girl came running after me to say that a big boy had been born and everything was fine, everyone was happy, and that I must soon come back for the baptism.

Of course I did return for the baptismal celebration. The boy was called Piotr (Peter); and I am sure that he was often told the story of his birth and baptism.

IN Poland, during the battle at the Narev, another medical experience began when a twenty-year-old girl, the eldest of ten children, came asking me to see her father, "although he is not worth it." She said he had evidently done something very shameful, because he had venereal disease.

I went, of course, and found the man with a very high fever and in a most serious condition that was not at all due to venereal disease. The poor man had been working in a swamp in bitter cold weather, and in some way his scrotum had been frozen and then given most unwise treatment. Now it was swollen to the size of a child's head. I gave him sulfonamide and vitamins, and treated the scrotum locally as well as I could.

Since I had the use of a horse at the time, I was able to visit the man whenever I visited any of the sick or wounded soldiers of my own unit who were housed in the neighborhood. When I came one day, all the family members were weeping. They uncovered the man and showed me that the greater part of the scrotum had fallen away. The testicles, however, were still intact. After some words to comfort the family, I made small interventions and cleansed away all the bad material.

When I got back to headquarters, I spoke with the army doctor about the case. Would it be possible, I asked, to make an artificial scrotum from the man's skin? The doctor became interested in the case and visited the patient. He said he had never seen such a cure attempted, but after talking with other experienced doctors, he was encouraged to try out the idea. We planned, then, that together we would do the job. But meanwhile mother nature herself was working, and a healing process began which made the surgery unnecessary. Soon the man was on the road to a good recovery. The testicles withdrew into the body, and the parts of the scrotum that were still intact began to grow.

Before the man was fully healed, however, the great Russian offensive began and we had to withdraw hastily from the area. I made a short visit to his home to say goodbye to him and his family. With tears, he said, "You are twice my father. My father gave me physical life; you have given life back to me and also given back to me the love and trust of my family. I was lost to them, but now I have life and health and my family, when I had thought there was no hope any more."

[4]

True Worshipers of God

From simple, unlettered Russian people I learned much about true worship of God: not worship taught by "specialists" in religion but that "worship in spirit and truth" of which our Lord spoke.

On some occasions I participated in the solemn liturgy of the Russian Orthodox Church, and observing there the marvelous liturgical dialogue of priest, deacon, and people, and the enthusiastic rendition of their music and hymns, I became convinced of the need to promote the vernacular in the Roman Catholic Church. However, that was not what most impressed me. The most impressive revelation was the spirit of faith that I found among humble people, even those who for many years had not enjoyed contact with any priest.

Early in February of 1943, when the battle around Stalingrad had come to an end, I had to undertake a long and dangerous trek with a number of wounded men, seeking shelter and food wherever we could find good people along the way. We came one day to a house in a little village

where a Russian family had saved the life of a German
soldier. Earlier, about a hundred German soldiers had been
captured, and the Russians, who came with tanks, could not
transport them and therefore had killed them. This one man
had been left seemingly dead. The family had discovered
that he was alive and had taken him into their house and
cared most kindly for him.

They were very glad when I came and could help him.
"Now you have to take him along with your other men,"
they said, "for his mother at home is surely praying to see
him again."

"But how can I take a man so badly wounded with me?"
I asked. I have no more space on the sleighs, and the horses
are worn out."

Even as we talked, another formation of Russian tanks
was approaching the village. "We will give you our
horses," these people said; and in no time they had har-
nessed their horses, carried the man to the sleigh, and sent
us off. It was faith, truly lived, that was manifested in this
incredible and risky generosity.

Three nights later my wounded friends and I were enjoy-
ing the hospitality of an aged couple. They gave us the last
of their bread and prepared a marvelous meal of potatoes
with salt and onions. It was all they had. More important
was the kindness they showed toward the sick men. I said,
"You are so kind as to give us your last piece of bread,
although we are people of an alien nation that has brought
great suffering to your country. May I ask why you do?"

The old gentleman answered. "In times of starvation,"
he said, "I was working in the mines, and after losing my
job I had to walk home several hundred miles. Day by day
on that long journey, someone would share his bread with
me, and I made a vow to God that I would never refuse
hospitality to anyone in need of it."

This was the mark of the Orthodox believer: that he would share his bread, knowing that he could not receive the Bread of Life if he would not share his own bread with others. In a time when they could not partake of the Eucharist, since they had no priest, they kept spiritual contact with the "breaking of the heavenly bread" by sharing their daily bread in generosity.

Two or three nights later, in another home, the same group of wounded men were received almost like sons of the family. I was completely exhausted, unable even to think about caring for the men or the horses. Immediately, the family took charge and then stayed up through the whole night to care for us.

In the morning they woke us up cheerfully. Until that time, no word had been spoken about faith. But before leaving I said, "You have treated us as if we were your sons. Tell us, why did you do it?" And it was the mother of the family who explained with great simplicity, "We have four sons in the Russian army, and each day we pray to our Father in heaven to bring them home healthy and safe. How could we dare to pray to him again today if we had forgotten that your father and mother, your family and friends, are praying to the same Father for the same thing?"

Then I told them, "I am a priest." When they heard that, tears came to their eyes. They said, "And you come to us and do not even give us your blessing? Why did you not let us know that you are a priest?"

I explained that I would not want to profit by it but would rather tell it only when I had experienced the faith of those whom I met. "And you have surely proved that you are Orthodox in your faith and in your life."

Not only was I touched by the living, active faith of these humble Russian people, I also learned how much a people with no theological training knew about prayer.

I arrived one day, very tired and dirty, in the Russian town of Kurganja, where our unit had been transferred from a station about fifteen miles distant. A family there, consisting of a great-grandmother, a grandmother, and the mother of a little child, tendered me a most affectionate welcome. I was hardly inside the door when the great-grandmother came to say, "Dear guest, the sauna (bath) is ready for you." When I was clean, I introduced myself as a priest.

They said, "We know it already, Father. We have heard about you and about your help for the sick people in the villages." Then they asked, "Would you mind if, in the evening, we would come together for prayer, and would you also talk to us on the gospel?" And the great-grandmother told me that through all the years when they had no priest she had been prayer leader for a group which came together regularly to pray and to talk about their faith.

That evening I experienced how a group of people kept their faith in times of persecution. And there I heard many questions about faith and manifestations of faith which were so deep and so relevant to life that later I sometimes told my students, "The illiterate people of Russia have asked more profound questions than you."

Not only in their daily living did these simple people manifest their faith. They evidenced it at times even to the point of martyrdom.

For a few weeks during our second winter in Russia, we

were stationed in a town named Nagolnoye. My quarters were in a house where a widow with six children lived in extreme poverty. I shall not easily forget these wonderful people. I even remember the beautiful Russian prayers they taught me. Their story was told to me by a holy woman, a school teacher who, in spite of all the pressures from the Communists, the risks, and the discrimination she had to endure, continued openly to confess her faith.

Some time earlier the Communists had summoned all the adult males one day and told them that they should "freely" decide to destroy the church in reparation for all the time they had wasted there. The men were all opposed, and in punishment for their dissent about one-third of the town's men were taken away to an unknown destiny and never heard from again. Among them was the husband of this good widow, father of her six children. Like the other victims, he was truly a martyr, and his wife and children considered him as such.

Some months later, the representatives of the militant atheists came again, and again the people gave witness to their faith. So a second third of the male population disappeared. Then finally the church was destroyed, after all. I saw the ruins, a mute testimony to the story.

The courtesy and kindness of these persecuted people was almost beyond belief. It happened that while I was living there a sergeant who was being transferred gave me a few chickens he owned. When I tried to give them to my hosts, I had a hard time to persuade them to accept the gift, although they were almost dying of starvation. Even on occasions when I wanted to share a part of my meal with the children, they showed themselves more concerned for me than I was for them.

Eᴀʀʟʏ in the spring of 1942, we were in a rather quiet corner near Kursk, where I had excellent relations with the Russian civilians. Through them I met their priest, and thereafter we met regularly. Sometimes he came to me; sometimes I visited him and his beautiful family. I asked him once how he had survived the difficult years. "Oh, God was so good to me!" he said. "I was in jail only three times and each time for less than a year." He paused then and sighed deeply. "But sometimes I had to eat meat in Lent, and also they cut my hair." (The Russian priests always wore long hair as a sign of their dignity).

The Orthodox church in the town had long since been dismantled by the Communist regime and used as a barn. I offered the priest my own and my friends' help to repair it so that it could be opened again for the liturgy. His first reaction was gratitude and readiness to accept the offer. But after discussing the matter with his friends, the elders, he told me that he could not accept, "because the German army will be defeated and the Communists will be back. Then everyone who cooperated with the opening of the church would be penalized." So he would prefer to live as he had to live under the Communist regime, and be able to baptize the children and to bring the last comfort to the dying believers.

Sᴏᴏɴ after my arrival in one little town, a gentleman presented himself to me as the sacristan of the church—a church which had been destroyed some twelve years before. He told me that he had saved the sacred vestments and chalices since that time. But immediately after telling me this, he had a question for me: did I recite the rosary? I showed him my rosary, and he was very disappointed.

I asked why this sign of love for the Mother of God (the Russian expression means "dear Mother of God") disturbed him. His answer was, "Well, it accords with our faith to love and venerate Mary, but when our priest left for exile in Siberia before the church was destroyed, his last testament was that if, later on, priests should come from the west saying the rosary, they were not to be received because they would not be of the Orthodox faith.

It was only after considerable difficulty that I finally convinced the man that I was of the right faith and that, indeed, nothing essential divided us.

IN the same town a young lady came one day to ask me to attend her father who was ill. She told me only that he was sick; she did not mention anything about his religion. So when I went to him, I simply gave him some medication and made him as comfortable as possible, but did not speak about faith.

The following day, his three daughters came to see me. They told me then that their father was a deacon and was distressed that, although I had given him medical care, I had not comforted him in his faith, as he had expected.

Now, understanding his position, I returned immediately, and our meeting this time was a great joy for both of us. During the hard years under Stalin, this man had been an administrator of a communal farm, yet during all that time he had done a great deal of ministry, instructing people in the faith at considerable risk to himself.

When he died, we honored him with a Christian funeral.

[5]

Samaritan and Pharisee

WHEN dealing with self-righteous atheists—and even more so with self-righteous Christians—I am tempted to identify them with the eternal Pharisee. But with people who, through their own fault or the fault of others, are in great trouble, I am more aware of the central message of the gospel, "Be compassionate as your Father is compassionate" (Luke 6:36). Yet again and again, I find in myself the eternal conflict between the merciful Samaritan and the self-righteous Pharisee.

WHEN the German army had conquered Kharkov in the autumn of 1941, the office where I received the ambulant sick and wounded soldiers was in a large apartment where a rather wealthy lady lived. Her husband was away; apparently he had a good position in the Communist Party.

The lady tried at first to enchant my helper, an attractive young man, but met with no success. He disliked her and labeled her "the witch." Very soon the witch revealed herself as an experienced fortune-teller. As her room was next door to my office, I could note, with considerable disappointment, that many of our men, both Catholic and Protestant, who came regularly to worship, were coming with equal regularity to the fortune-teller.

The witch's ears were everywhere. Evidently she was quite skilled at gathering knowledge about her customers, which she would then display while "reading the cards" to these naïve fellows. More and more they were putting their faith in this nonsense and wasting their meagre pay on it. I could see, too, that their superficial knowledge of Russian, and the bit of German the witch spoke, helped her all the better to confuse them.

So I offered my services as interpreter for one of the sessions when all the men were there. In this new role I used some of the witch's own strategy of confusion, by inserting some indirect insinuations into the translation to mislead her. She promptly adopted the insinuations, but the men were still not clever enough to discover the trickery. Finally I inquired whether I, too, might ask a question. For her, this request seemed quite a triumph, since until then I had been obviously antipathetic.

I told her that since my arrival in Kharkov I had not received any letters, and that I was worried about whether my wife had written at all. The witch looked long at the cards, calculating carefully a response that would not be proven false. Finally she came up with the oracle's answer: "The cards do not tell me whether or when the letter will arrive. However, they do tell me that your wife is writing and has written regularly."

Of course I told her then that I had no wife, and told my credulous friends how she had been exploiting them. The effect was like an exorcism. She ran away angry, and the men finally woke up to the folly of looking for wisdom, knowledge, or help from such a source.

Samaritan and Pharisee

DURING our first winter in Russia, at a very advanced post where we had almost no connection with the rest of the army or with the military hospital, a soldier contracted syphilis. He was a bright but arrogant young fellow, a journalist by profession. As medic, I had to write a report to the commander and search for the source of contamination.

In such cases soldiers were required to identify the women with whom they had sexual relations. I was surprised when this young man named as his partner a woman well over forty, the mother of three children. She had been divorced some years before and, like many others in those harsh days, had resorted to this means of providing for her children. She was at heart a decent woman who had gone astray because of dire circumstances.

I had no sympathy whatever for the man and would have liked to give him a fire-and-brimstone sermon, but medics were forbidden to show any reaction in these cases; and besides, I knew it would do no good. So there was nothing left but to act as Samaritan, although an angry one, and give him the prescribed treatment. For the woman, I felt only sympathy, pity.

But when the commander received the report, he gave me strict orders to "do away with the woman!" That meant to kill her or have her killed, since there was no way to send her to a hospital or to take her into custody. I did not argue the order because I knew that if I expressed any conscientious objection he would simply give the order to someone else. I just hoped that, meeting no objection, he would not inquire further and the case would be closed if the woman did not show up any more as a source of contamination.

I then went to the woman and revealed what had happened. As gently as possible, I told her about the order I

35

had received, assuring her all the while that she would not be killed or otherwise punished if she would follow the rules for a cure and take the medicines regularly. But I warned her that if she contaminated another soldier, my life as well as hers would be in danger. The woman gratefully accepted the therapy and promised not to make any trouble for anyone, and I knew that I could trust her promise.

Thereafter, whenever I passed by on my visits to the sick and saw her, she spontaneously renewed her promise, "Never again!" And I noted that somehow her children got their daily bread after all, without their mother being exploited.

FROM the end of February until April of 1943, our unit was being recomposed in Orel, a town southwest of Moscow. I was quartered with two medical helpers and some sick soldiers in a relatively large house occupied by three families.

One of the families was Natasha's, a refugee, mother of three children, and utterly destitute. To obtain food for herself and her children, she had finally begun to sell the only thing she had left, her body.

My two medical helpers—both unbelievers, but both also severe moralists—realized what Natasha's business was and told me how they intended to stop it. They would open the door each time someone came, and would pour a pail of water over every man, whether German or Russian, who came to "visit" Natasha. As medical sergeant, however, I had to forbid this method in the terrible cold of winter. "Well, then," they said, "take care of the situation yourself, since you will not allow us to do it our way."

So I went to Natasha and told her that if she would refuse everyone who wanted to exploit her, I would provide her daily food: I would give her part of mine and invite the Russian people who needed my medical care to contribute also.

Natasha gladly promised, but time and again, people would come knocking at her door. I remember one whom I intercepted, a Russian who worked in the German army. I explained to him quietly that Natasha was no longer in such misery that she had to be exploited by people like him, and I admonished him to give up such ideas. He answered that he had no intention of changing his mind; he felt this was his right. I made my argument stronger, but to no avail. Finally I lost my temper and shouted at him in Bavarian dialect. My bellow and the alien tongue accomplished what my good arguments had not. Frightened, he ran away as if the devil himself were behind him.

Altogether, I was a little too satisfied about my kindness to Natasha. I felt I was the merciful Samaritan. But it was a case of pride before the fall.

Some days before Easter I asked Natasha if, now that the snow had gone, she could help to clean things around the house. At that time in Russia, outside the cities there were no toilets in the houses. Even during the most severe winter, people had to go outdoors when nature called. The consequence was that after the long winters there was much cleaning to be done around the houses, and it was truly slavish work.

Natasha apologized politely—and maybe with a little too much confidence—that she would do it after Easter if nobody else could do it, but that now she needed all her time to make shoes for herself and her children because she wanted to go to church on Easter eve. Taking her excuse as a sign of laziness or unwillingness to do her share of the dirty work, I exploded, "What are people like you doing in church if they do not want to work?"

It is hard to say who was more shocked by this outburst, Natasha or myself. Natasha had believed that she had met someone who honored and respected her. And now? A flood of tears answered the Pharisee; and I, in a rush of contrition and remorse, apologized immediately. Natasha could justly have lashed me with my own question but she forgave me instead. On Easter eve, she went to church and brought back to me the blessed bread, salt, and egg, a most gracious sign of reconciliation.

ARE there hopeless sinners? Some think so, and sometimes I, too, have been tempted to consider a few people as hopeless cases. But in a lifetime I have seen the truth the gospel teaches so clearly: Christ has not written anyone off as a hopeless sinner.

In close contact with soldiers, I knew a lot about their faults and about the bad characters of some. Yet when it was a question of life and death, I could suddenly discover the real person: one ready to accept pain and death, ready to believe in divine forgiveness and the possibility of repentance.

One of my most astonishing experiences was to discover how great is the impact of a healthy—and unfortunately also of an unhealthy—environment, and to realize that this transforming environment can be created by only one or two good and generous people. I am reminded of a change, by no means world-shaking but none the less delightful, that I saw in a group of rough men when they came into an environment created by a few gentle, devoted nuns.

In May, 1942, on a day of terrible fighting, when my five medical helpers had already been lost, I was wounded. And since my situation was serious, I was sent back to Germany on a hospital train. On the journey, most of the men around me were soldiers of an SS unit—shallow, rather coarse fellows who, in spite of their grave wounds, were already dreaming of playing around with the pretty nurses and other girls whom they would find in the military hospital.

When we arrived in Dillingen, Bavaria, however, their disappointment was great: they discovered that all the nurses in the big ward which we were to occupy were nuns! Yet very soon the whole atmosphere changed radically, because every one of the thirty soldiers, including the SS men, admired and loved the nuns, especially the one who was the head nurse. If anyone used obscene language or cursed, as soon as he became aware of it he would look to see if Sister had heard it, and would apologize. Or his neighbor would say, "I hope Sister did not hear you."

Courtesy grew, mutual help and encouragement grew, the whole microcosmic room changed. And the sisters continued with their loving, happy service as if nothing remarkable were happening, as if they had known all along how much goodness was in these men.

[6]

Not Quite Like Christ

AN interesting and worthwhile study could be made about the difficulties of adapting to an environment very different from one's earlier one; and indeed it is hard to imagine two environments more diverse than that of the monastery major seminary where I had studied and taught for seven years and the rough environment of Hitler's army.

All my training, from childhood to priesthood, had made me keenly aware of my mission and obligation, both as a Christian and as a priest, to give witness to my religious convictions and to the freedom of the sons and daughters of God. It had also stressed nonviolence and gentleness: virtues that have nothing to do with weakness.

My rule of adaptation on entering the military service was, therefore, that I would treat most courteously those who themselves were gentle and courteous, and would serve anyone, Christians and non-Christians alike, who needed my help; but whoever would disparage my beliefs would receive from me a fitting response. Yet looking back today, I have to ask myself how "fitting" some of my responses were. Did they really fit my obligation to witness as Christian and priest, or did they fit only the offense, or even only my irascible mood of the moment?

M Y first combative response took place in Augsburg during my training course for the army medical corps. While many of the students there were good Catholics, others were of quite a different type. One of them, a strongly built butcher from southern Bavaria, asked a favor of me. He said that he had no money to pay the bus fare from the hospital where he worked to the dormitory, and asked if I would lend him money for a week. In my naïvete I agreed to do so.

A day or two later, I came upon a group of soldiers who were having some fun. They did not see me coming. My butcher borrower, Haggemeyer by name, was in their midst, telling them that with the money he had borrowed from "the priest" he had gone to the *Hasengasse,* a well-known haunt of prostitutes. When I heard what he had done with my money, and especially that he was boasting before others that he had done it with money lent by a priest, I was seized with tremendous wrath. I rushed at him and took him by the throat. "This moment," I demanded, "you give me back that money; I did not lend it to you to tell stories like this!"

Shaken, he had to beg his companions, who had found his story so amusing a moment before, to give him money to repay me. They did, and I left him then to face all the embarrassment of his reduced status.

D URING our stay in Russia, a soldier was repeatedly insulting, in coarse and primitive language, the Church and all

Christian believers. I warned him to show a little more sense and better manners, or at least not to make such a show of his stupidity. The fellow became furious and wanted to knock me down. He was a strong young man, but he had miscalculated. He did not know how well my own physical energies had been strengthened by carrying wounded men and otherwise doing a medic's job. So he was the one who found himself on the ground. Not without sarcasm, I invited him to stand up, assuring him that I would not defile myself any more by touching him.

Strangely enough, this man became quite a friend of mine. He was later transferred to another unit and we did not see each other for two years. But on the very day our army surrendered and we became war prisoners, he saw me and ran to greet and embrace me. And he thanked me again, as he had during the time of our friendship, for putting him on the right path.

ANOTHER show of anger was more a seriously played comedy than a quarrel. It occurred just after the plot against Hitler had failed, and we had all been given orders to salute thereafter with "Heil Hitler." A group of soldiers were there, and a thoughtless young fellow said, to the great amusement of the others, "Look at Father Häring; he is really in despair because the plot against Hitler failed!"

I knew that the young man did not mean to harm me, but his remark could mean a trial for me and even the loss of my life. So I called him out and berated him like a Prussian officer, finally commanding him to walk through a rather juicy dunghill. He had to obey the command. When we were alone later I asked, "Did you understand, my friend, why I had to do that?" He agreed that he did understand,

". . . and I appreciate your making a comedy of it instead of being really angry with me."

ONE of our most horrible times was on our forced retreat from the Narev early in 1945. We had lost most of our motorized vehicles. Relying only on undernourished and tired horses, we had to carry a part of our luggage; yet within less than two weeks we were forced back more than three hundred miles, stopping from time to time to attempt useless counterattacks. There were casualties from freezing as well as from battle.

Often the roads were blocked by the stream of German-speaking or part-German civilians who, fearing that the Russians would kill them or rape their wives and daughters, were trying to escape from the area. In the bitter cold they had suddenly to leave their homes, packing whatever they could on their huge carts. Soon their horses were unable to move on the slippery roads. Impatient soldiers—either to save their own lives or to move in an orderly fashion—were simply taking the horses from the refugees or forcing their carts off the road, where they got hopelessly stuck.

At one point I was trying to help a family with several small children to get their cart back on the road, when one of the German soldiers whom I had asked to make room for the cart gave me several sharp lashes with his whip. Furious, I sprang onto his cart and, taking him by the neck, I held him so that he could hardly breathe, much less call for help. Only when the family had at last got their cart back and moving on the road did I give him his freedom, along with an angry warning not to repeat his despicable behavior.

NEAR the end of the war, when the city of Danzig was already occupied by the Russians, we were in a large forest behind the city. The doctor and I were ministering to a number of wounded soldiers when a colonel came along, raging against the "cowards" who would not fight.

Realizing that he was one of the chief judges who had sentenced hundreds of good German soldiers to death because they saw no sense in the unreasonable prolongation of a lost war—or, in some cases, only because they had become "displaced persons," lost from their units—I completely lost my temper. I turned on him, shouted at him, calling him a criminal and whatever else came to mind. The doctor and the soldiers around me stood aghast, their faces white, thinking that I would be the next one to hang. However, the colonel himself turned pale when he saw my fury, and disappeared.

I am sure that he would have taken quick revenge if he had not realized the terrible revenge the men would have taken on him if he took any drastic steps against me at that moment. But I am still amazed that I got away unscathed after such an outburst.

WHILE I do not truly repent these actions, I would be happy if I could have done the same things without such enormous wrath.

In the intervening years when I have spoken—in South Africa, Rhodesia, Brazil, and elsewhere—about nonviolent action and the victory of gentleness, people have often reminded me of the wrath of Jesus in the temple. My usual response has been that I understand that wrath all too well, but we should be aware that we do not at all match the discretion of Christ; therefore we cannot allow ourselves to judge others. And finally, we have not his authority and could easily become abusive.

THERE were also less pugnacious confrontations. At the beginning of the war against Russia, I was sent to a battalion of infantrymen. When I came to the door of the little Russian house where the commander of the battalion had his quarters, I heard uproarious laughter. He and his fellow officers were joking about the news that a priest was coming to serve as medical sergeant.

I knocked at the door and presented myself. The officer made an extravagant show of welcoming me, expressing great happiness at seeing me, and saying that they were all honored to have a Catholic priest "and even a professor of theology!" who would surely give the best possible service. I responded coolly enough that only the future would prove which of his words were sincere: those I had just heard before I could knock at the door, or the words he was speaking now. I said I would like to have good rapport with them all, but only on terms of sincerity.

In the future, this man left me in peace, not because he respected Catholic priests but because he was aware that he would meet a challenge. Gradually we became friends, since he really did appreciate my service as medic, and he himself was a competent commander.

ANOTHER officer in our battalion at that time was a quite aggressive and offensive atheist. He attacked me repeatedly about my religious convictions, and each time I responded in kind.

He sent a messenger one day, ordering me to come to see him because he did not feel well. Knowing that he was not really sick, I told the messenger, "If he is very sick I will come to see him. If he is not very sick he should come to see me as everyone else does." He promptly reported this to the commander who, fortunately, considered his complaint too trivial to bother with.

Some time later this man was gravely wounded in a big battle. He cried for help and, though it was risky enough to move, I ran to help him, and carried him away on my shoulders. I still remember his surprise at my willingness to do this duty as if nothing had happened between us.

ONCE when a soldier expressed, before me and one of our officers, his contempt for the Catholic Church and for priests, I did not respond to the fellow himself but turned to the officer who, I knew, was an atheist. I asked if he, as an officer, would allow one of his men to insult the religious convictions of another man without a reprimand. Did he not have the duty, as a man of honor, to ask the man to apologize? Taken by surprise, the officer did, indeed, require the man to apologize.

WHAT I learned from my experience in the German army was that people of low morality and a low level of respect for another's convictions are always ready to persecute those who do not have the courage to resist; but if they meet strong and confident resistance, they learn to respect, at least to the point of silence, the other's position.

Ordinarily, any difficulty I had with soldiers or officers happened only when I first came to a unit or when a new group came to ours. When we had lived together for a longer time, everyone knew that I would give help to whoever needed it but would not tolerate any contemptuous attitude toward my faith.

[7]

The Path to Peace
and the Road to Perdition

No task is more urgent for both society and the Church, and particularly for moral theologians, than concern for peace.

I think it was God's providence that I had to go through the horrors and hardships of the Second World War in order to become more sharply aware that the gospel of our Lord Jesus Christ is, above all, a message of peace and of the path to peace. A disciple of Christ can be defined as a person who gratefully receives the gift of divine peace and thereby is thoroughly committed to the mission of reconciliation and peace on all levels.

The war years offered me some personal experiences of how we can serve the cause of peace, and some lessons of what constitute the main threats to peace and the main causes of war and perdition.

WHEN we first entered the Ukraine at the beginning of the war against Russia, the population received us in a way that was not only friendly but almost triumphant, as if we were liberators. People were in the streets when we entered their villages, offering milk, bread, honey, strawberries, and other fine things to our exhausted men. Their excessive hopes had been kindled especially by the war prisoners of the First World War who had spent years in Germany, mostly as workers on farms. These ex-prisoners spoke well of Germans, and the people therefore expected all of us to be like those old German farmers of whom the veterans spoke so frequently and so favorably.

During the first four weeks our division did not suffer any great losses—although even our relatively small losses were dreadful. We treated the prisoners well, and the people's expectations rose even higher. Repeatedly I heard them speak among themselves when they did not know that I understood them. During those first weeks, doctors and medical helpers generally did what they were obliged to do by conscience and international agreements. We gave the wounded Russian soldiers as much care as the hurried movements of our army allowed.

Then in the fourth week, two SS regiments were inserted into the same part of the front. These criminals soon began to kill their prisoners and to refuse any treatment to wounded Russian soldiers and civilians. Immediately, the attitude of the population toward us changed. Now people were friendly only to those of us whom they had begun to know as honest and decent men.

The message must have spread quickly among the Russian soldiers, for now they offered real resistance. Within one week we suffered more losses than in the previous four weeks, and the number of Russian prisoners dropped sharply. Those who surrendered were frightened, and it took a lot of kindly talk to assure them that they would be treated as human beings. As far as our regiment was concerned, this was still true.

It was unfortunate, too, that so few of our men spoke Russian. In our whole regiment I was the only one; and since I therefore had to serve as interpreter on all occasions, I quickly became fluent in the language. Wherever people can talk with each other, share their joys, hopes, sufferings, and anxieties, the relationships change rapidly for the better; there is less temptation to do injustice to each other through contemptuous judgments or harmful actions.

In the different units in which I served and in their various compositions, I came across all kinds of attitudes and mixtures of behavior. I was sometimes terribly disappointed in some of my soldier friends, even a few who came to worship. Normally, when we were a long time in one place, the Russian people would become quite friendly with me because of my medical help, and especially because I was a priest. Then some of the men who associated with me would, on that account, also gain the people's friendship. Yet on several occasions when we were leaving a place, they did not resist the temptation to steal something from these poor people. I was terribly grieved whenever I learned of this, and rebuked the men severely.

Those of our men who took their Christian faith seriously, who came regularly to meditations and to worship, frequently expressed their anguish of conscience about participating in this unjustified war. My constant advice to them was not to kill, not to rob or steal, but rather to protect the civilians and to show kindness and friendship to the prisoners. For the infantrymen, however, my advice "do not kill" was not as easy as for me. I had decided to forego public conscientious objection, although I admired those who made it their cause. My preference was to be with the sick and wounded, to try to heal in the midst of horror. But for those engaged in the actual fighting, the conflict was much sharper, and I saw how deeply some of the men were afflicted by what they were going through.

DURING our first winter in Russia, our regiment was stationed for several weeks in a large village named Mal Psinka where, for at least two weeks, we were out of touch with the rest of the army. Throughout the time, I took care of our own men as well as the wounded Russian prisoners who could still be helped. I also attended the sick and wounded among the Russian civilians. Many families had generously put their houses at the disposal of these war victims, and day by day I visited as many as possible.

Thank God, I had enough medicine, and no doubt the robust health of the Russians contributed greatly to their very good rate of recovery. Soon these good people were putting almost unlimited trust in me and were calling me "the doctor," although I explained often enough that I had only partial training and, in any event, could work no miracles. Their good recoveries, I told them, were due to the quality of the medicines I dispensed and to the fact that their splendid powers of resistance had not been weakened by the use of all kinds of drugs.

When we had again made contact with the rest of the army, I was called for a hearing before the regiment's new commander. I was accused of having squandered army medical supplies by serving so many Russian prisoners and civilians.

The colonel—a righteous man although he had earlier served in the SS—asked for my version of the facts. I easily justified myself by proving that, through the Russian friends I had made by serving their sick and wounded, I had learned of enormous quantities of medical supplies left behind by the Russian army. These I had collected, thereby greatly increasing the German supply. The colonel not only absolved me of the accusation but acknowledged that my help to the Russians was a genuine help also to the army since, because of it, the people were more friendly toward our own soldiers.

A few weeks after our stay in Mal Psinka, our unit had to be restored because we had lost so many men. We were brought to a small Russian town about twenty miles from the front, where I was accommodated, along with some of the sick men, in the rather spacious house of the mayor of the town.

The mayor and I soon became friends, free to speak frankly with each other about the war situation. He told me what I, as a German, had already experienced: that when the Germans first came, many people in his country had greeted them as liberators from despotism, but they soon became terribly disillusioned because of the crimes committed by Hitler's men and the bad behavior of many German officers and officials. "Now we look upon the German army as a colonial power," he said, "and if we have to choose between tyrants, we do better to keep our own rather than yield to colonial despots."

While we were talking in this vein one evening, he remarked, ". . . but if all the German officers would treat our people like the doctor in Mal Psinka, I am sure the war would go differently." The reference to the "doctor in Mal Psinka" caught me by surprise, and I asked, "Do you know this doctor personally?" He said, "Unfortunately I do not, but everyone has heard about how generously he cared for our Russian soldiers and civilians there." Somewhat embarrassed, I then confessed my identity. I told him, however, that while I very much appreciated his praise, my services were only what everyone should expect under the circumstances, in accordance with international agreements and mere human sensitivity.

This man's observation that with humane treatment "the war would go differently" remains in my mind. But the oppressor mentality is unable to grasp this truth.

An incident in this same context can illustrate the conflicting attitudes that existed among soldiers and officers, and sometimes even in one and the same person.

When the colonel who absolved me in the case of the medical supplies first came to our regiment, he was known to be an unbeliever and a strict disciplinarian. Consequently, in the first days under his command, I did not dare to organize public religious services for the soldiers. Yet when several of the men went to him and complained that there was no chaplain and no pastoral care for them, he respected their feelings and encouraged me to exercise my ministry. I am sure he knew that the law forbade it.

As a disciplinarian, however, he tightened the supervision of the wounded Russian prisoners of war for whom I was caring and who were housed with various families in the village. Taking care of these men as I did, and hearing about their lives, their families, and their homes, it was natural that personal relationships developed. Hence, I was not at all unhappy when some of them silently disappeared as soon as they had recovered. Now, under the new discipline, these escapes were hardly possible.

When a group of about twenty prisoners was restored to sufficient health, the colonel gave orders to bring them to a station behind the front for transportation to a prison camp. Our men took the prisoners to this station and handed them over to those responsible for their further transport. But a young officer there greeted the German soldiers with contempt. "You stupid louts!" he cried. "Why these long marches? Can't you dispose of these Russians yourselves?" And he and one of his fellows immediately began to shoot the prisoners.

When our soldiers, still filled with horror, came back and reported all this to the colonel, he was as filled with wrath as the rest of us. From that moment, there was no more question of control over the wounded Russian soldiers. Their disposal was practically left to me. This meant that they usually found some civilian clothes and just became a part of the civilian population, free either to venture on their way home or to wait for better times.

Sometimes our unit suffered losses from partisans. Once, two or three men who seemed to be dangerous partisans were captured. The colonel asked one of our officers whether he had a man who would shoot the partisans in the neck. When he received a prompt yes, he was angry. Although he was a tough man, he had hoped that nobody would be ready to follow such an order, even if he passed it on.

It might seem that the following stories about war crimes are nothing compared to the destruction of millions of Jews and Gypsies in Hitler's death camps, to the bombing of Coventry—or the continued bombing of open towns by both sides—to dropping the A-bombs on Hiroshima and Nagasaki, or to the records compiled in the Nuremberg trials. If everyone were to be judged by the norms of human justice, there would be almost no end to the accusations and convictions of war criminals. But I wish to share these particular stories because they illustrate, even though on a relatively small scale, the broad road to perdition; and perhaps we can learn, even from this negative aspect, something about how to prepare the path to peace.

I shall never forget one horrifying experience in Kharkov around the middle of November, 1941. We had been at a meeting of friends, mostly priests and brothers of various religious orders. As we were returning to our quarters, we heard announcements blaring everywhere that the Jews of the city were to be resettled and must come next morning, with all their belongings, to another part of the city. I still had time to warn some of my Jewish friends in the neighborhood not to show up but rather to go into hiding, because I very much distrusted the whole idea of "resettling."

The next evening one of my friends, a Catholic soldier, came to me thoroughly disturbed, babbling nonsense, crying, weeping. Finally I could understand what had happened. He had been ordered, with other soldiers, to kill the Jews who had reported for "resettlement." The suddenness of the order so surprised him that he had obeyed; but when it was over he almost lost his mind and came to me seeking help in his terrible distress.

Some days later, my medical helper came home almost equally disturbed. He had not participated in any execution but he had just seen the bodies of Jews being packed on lorries. It was the first time he had seen or even heard of such atrocities. Like most of the soldiers, he had been completely uninformed about the magnitude of the crimes that were going on in the Third Reich.

All our soldiers who had heard about the massacre of the Jews were stricken at the thought that their military service was involving them in these inhuman acts.

The Path to Peace and the Road to Perdition

In a Russian village in January of 1942, our battalion was under repeated heavy attacks from strong Russian forces. We could hold the village only because we all knew that to be driven out meant probable death in the snowfields. Our casualties were high, and since there was no physician with us, the whole responsibility for the wounded and sick soldiers and civilians rested on me. Many of the wounded needed surgery or more intensive care in a military hospital but we had no means of transport. Besides, our isolation was complete since all the neighboring villages were in the hands of the Russian army. The nearest German evacuation hospital was at least twenty miles distant.

Through my work with their sick and wounded, I had come to know many of the Russian civilians. They trusted me and shared my grave concern about the wounded men who should be hospitalized. On their own initiative, they finally told me that they had been hiding sleighs and horses —indeed, the Russians were real experts at hiding a few vital belongings—and they would be willing to help me transport the patients to the hospital if they could be sure that their horses would not then be confiscated. They knew the roads and knew how to avoid the Russian-held villages.

I then went to the commander of the battalion, a man whom I thought I could trust, and presented, hypothetically, a plan for getting sleighs and horses from the Russian civilians if I could assure them that these properties would not later be confiscated by the army. The commander assured me that in this case—which he did not consider actual —there would be no confiscation. So now I could approach the village elders and speak seriously about the plan.

They got together eight or nine sleighs and the right number of horses, and the Russian owners of the horses then ventured on this dangerous enterprise with me and only one of my helpers. We were unarmed. Our caravan moved silently all through the icy night. When we arrived at the evacuation hospital the next morning, the doctors could hardly believe that we had made such a journey. They treated us well, giving us warm food and a place to rest. The following night we drove back, again in silence, to our village.

When we arrived there I learned, to my horror and utter dismay, that the commander had reverted to the war mentality and decided to confiscate the horses and sleighs. "The battalion needs them," he said. And although he said it with visible regret, did he not realize that mankind, and especially we in that situation, needed, above all, mutual trust?

I was so ashamed before my Russian friends that their goodness had been so incredibly abused, that I was glad when very soon we moved on to another village. To this day I am heartsick when I remember this infamous betrayal. It was, after all, only a mirror image of all the misdeeds in the world that destroy the possibility of mutual confidence and thus of peace.

In 1943, we were stationed for some time in the village of Kurgania. A beautiful large church stood there, and the people told me the story of its preservation.

When, in 1929 and again in 1933, the Communist laws had become more severe and the taxes for the church increased, hundreds of people not only gave their names as members of the church but also contributed large sums for the taxes. Some even sold their last cow in order to keep the church. The law allowed—and still allows—a parish to operate if the required number of people sign as parish members. Of course this is not only a profession of faith for those who sign but also a risk that exposes them to political pressures and discrimination. Twenty years before, the Communist regime had exiled the priest, and the people had no church services, but they had faithfully kept the church through all those years.

We were still stationed here when the war situation became such that Hitler had to withdraw several divisions from Russia. One evening, our commander called me by phone, telling me that he had a horrible headache. But it was not a physical one. He had learned from a general that an order had been given to destroy all the towns and villages in the zones that would be evacuated. The commander then had a terrible confrontation with the general and shouted, "Are we soldiers or are we criminals?" But the general, too, was a sensitive man and had begun to weep in bitter despair.

The next morning technicians from other groups came into the town and began to undermine the church. The officer in charge of these men said it had to be destroyed because it could serve as an observation post for the enemy. The rest of the village was also to be destroyed.

The time came when the soldiers and the whole civilian population had to leave the area for the moment when the church would be blown up. I was in the midst of the civilians when the dreadful event occurred. Seldom in my life have I witnessed a similar explosion of pain, suffering, and despair. What Stalin had not achieved, the Nazi barbarians completed.

IN the Pripet Palude area where we were stationed in the spring of 1944, the poverty was so extreme that lives could depend upon the milk from a single cow. Yet a group of German soldiers, under command of a certain Captain

Wöhrle, would steal cows, perhaps the last ones in a neighborhood, two or three times a week. As we were fairly well provided with food, it was not to assuage hunger but only to enjoy something extra.

On one occasion the people had organized in self-defence and had killed three of the soldier-thieves who had been sent by this godless scoundrel. The official information sent back to the families of these soldiers was that they had been killed in a fight against partisans.

I had studied in this captain's home town and knew that he was a member of a good Christian family. However, he had become involved with the Nazi youth movement and had given up his faith in God. When, in 1946, I heard that he was home and studying law, I went to his parents' house to confront him. He was not at home, so I left a message with his brother that I would be at the railroad station the next day at a certain time, and he should not fail to meet me there. He did come, trembling as if he were freezing. I told him, "You were one of the worst law-breakers in the worst of times, and you were responsible for the lives of innocent people. I tell you now that you cannot be a protector of the law. You are to stop studying law and take some other job where you will have no such responsibility for the common good." He knew well that I meant what I said and that I could be a credible witness against him. He did not contradict me.

His was one of two cases which I had determined to pursue when the war was over. The other was that of a general who had been stealing chalices and other church properties in Poland. However, that general was, to my knowledge, condemned by the Russians.

IN that part of Poland's western provinces to which we had withdrawn early in 1945, the majority of the population spoke both Polish and German, while a minority spoke only German. When the battlefront broke open and the fighting came to this area, the German-speaking farmers tried to flee with their livestock and whatever other possessions they could transport.

It all told of the curse of the Prussian empire's colonialism which had, again and again, sent settlers in to germanize those areas of Poland. Now, in the turmoil of war, these people had to bear a part of the burden of the sins of their forefathers. The terrible suffering was hitting the innocent along with the guilty. Even many who had only the German name of one grandparent, and who felt solidarity with the Polish people, had to flee and were later exiled by the Communist regime.

Yet it must be admitted that among them there were some who had indulged in quite serious discrimination and injustice against the Polish people. I saw, myself, a little indication of this attitude. My quarters at the time were in a huge barn belonging to a rich German family who were quite friendly to me during the first days. When, however, I returned on the following Sunday, after saying mass for the soldiers in the home of a Polish Catholic family, I heard members of the German family and some of their neighbors expressing surprise that "Feldwebel Häring, too, is a *Polak.*" That I was Catholic and celebrated mass in a Polish home made me, in their eyes, Polish, and therefore somehow inferior.

I mention this otherwise insignificant incident only because it points to an attitude typical of many places in the world today where national or economic interests and col-

61

lective egotisms are the real causes of trouble but are strangely mixed with religious rootedness and fanaticism. This is true, for instance, in northern Ireland and in Lebanon.

The suffering of the German-speaking people of western Poland was enormous. I have already told something of the flight of the refugees, driven in panic along the frozen roads. Like some of the refugees we could observe in the takeover of the Vietcong in Vietnam, they might have done better to have stayed in their homes.

One of the saddest memories of those hard days is of one terribly cold night when we were protecting ourselves in a huge unheated building where the presence of so many bodies—soldiers and refugees—made the temperature somehow bearable. A family came in very late, bringing their many children, coughing and crying. But when they brought in the youngest child, they found that he had frozen to death.

No memory can bear all the lamentation and expressions of despair that we witnessed in those days. They were truly apocalyptic, like the days predicted by our Lord for the fall of Jerusalem.

IN February of 1945, on about the eleventh day of our forced withdrawal from the Narev, the doctor and I had to stop for a while to take care of a number of sick and wounded men. After having brought them to a certain house and promised to return later to pick them up, we made our way through the snow in the late afternoon to join our unit.

On the road I saw a body, and thinking it was a soldier, I went to look for his identity card so that we could inform his family of his death. But it was not a soldier; it was a woman, killed by a shot in the neck. Then later, one by one, we came upon the bodies of about forty other women killed in the same way, still lying in the street, some of them not quite dead but in their last agony. The wrath in our hearts cannot be imagined when we realized that German Nazis had killed the women because they were Jewish.

When we finally caught up with our unit, our soldiers informed us, with the same wrath in their hearts and on their lips, that the dead women were Hungarian Jews who earlier had been forced to dig for the army which was then in retreat. Those who could not follow with the others were killed on the spot by a shot in the neck.

That night, we had to drive back to retrieve our wounded and sick. It was a horrifying experience to drive over that road trying to avoid the womens' bodies still lying there untended. The next morning, several of my soldier friends informed me that they had succeeded in hiding, in various houses of Polish civilians, some of the Jewish women who were sick. They asked if I would help the women, and I went with them immediately.

I found that I could take care of some of the injured or sick women myself, but in two or three cases some major surgery or even amputation was indicated. I therefore asked the doctor if he would assist me. His reluctant response was, "Father Häring, you are celibate; you expose only your own life. I am married and the father of three children, and have duties also to my own people. When you need some medical advice or other kind of help, I will give it to you, but do not ask me to visit these ladies and expose myself so immediately to the risk involved."

I still wonder, even now, if these persecuted women were saved. They told me that if they lived they would somehow find me after the war wherever my place on earth might be, but I never heard from them again. The SS heard about

them and came to the little town (Schlewitska) to seek
them. They did not find them on that occasion, for the
Polish population had hidden them well. Very soon the
Russian army took the town.

TOWARD the end of the war, almost all the soldiers in my
unit were against Hitler. Many groups even listened together to the enemy radio, all quite sure that none would
betray the other.

On the annual day of remembrance of the dead, I celebrated a mass very well attended, not only by the soldiers
but also by several officers. On that occasion I said the
prescribed prayer for the Fatherland and the authorities. I
did not mention the name of Hitler, but prayed for "those
who guide our country."

After the mass, a group of my friends came and gave me
an ultimatum: they would no longer assist at any mass of
mine if I would repeat any prayer for "that God-damned
fellow." They knew quite well my own feelings against
Hitler, but they felt that those feelings should be expressed
by never praying, even indirectly, for him.

THE closer the senseless war came to its end, the more
insane became the criminality of Hitler's obedient slaves. In
the disorderly withdrawal, many soldiers were scattered.
Perhaps some abandoned their units deliberately, hoping to
hide somewhere or to find the way home to their families.
In reaction to this situation, fast-working military tribunals
(Schnellgerichte) were set up everywhere, dealing out death
penalties, mostly by hanging, for those who were found
separated from their units.

A young cousin of mine, Alphons Flad, met me by chance

one day and begged me to get him into our unit. He had lost his company and was afraid of being hung if some military commando found him. He had a minor wound; so I told him I could do something even better for him. "There is a boat leaving soon with hundreds of seriously wounded. I can bring you there." This was one of the last satisfactions I had in those terrible days.

For a week or so, I was stationed in Oliva, a suburb of Danzig. When I brought some of the sick and wounded from there to the harbor, I had to pass through a long avenue lined with trees. On each tree hung some poor young fellow—many of them no more than children—decorated with a big placard reading, "I am a coward, a traitor; I did not want to fight."

Under heavy fire from Russian artillery and tanks, we finally had to retreat from Danzig. Our way led through another avenue of huge trees. It was winter; the trees had no leaves. But on each one were hanging bodies of German men, young and old, all with the same placard. It was a horrible sight. Our hearts were filled with despair and anger.

A Russian man who had agreed to do service in the German army rather than go to prison camp, and who probably had still hoped that something better than Stalin's Communism might come, said to me with great bitterness on that dismal day, "What's the point of this war now? Stalin could do this hanging as well as Hitler."

[8]

Freedom under Tyrants and Freedom under Law

ONE of the greatest experiences is this: to keep one's inner freedom under tyrants and to find as many occasions as possible to manifest this freedom in words and actions.

It seems to me that oppression, although it is abominable, can be a stimulating challenge to explore more actively all the dimensions of freedom and to discern better between true freedom and its counterfeits. The more we meet this challenge, the more we appreciate freedom and commit ourselves to promote it at all levels and for all people.

Looking back, I see the difficult experiences of the war as a hard school for discovering the unique value of freedom of conscience, the right meaning of responsibility and responsible obedience, as well as a more mature approach to law, including church law. For the question must be asked: Could so many people have been so easily manipulated by totalitarian regimes if they had been prepared for discernment and growth in freedom rather than trained for order and obedience?

Although B. F. Skinner, author of *Beyond Freedom and Dignity,* does not recognize the value of either freedom or dignity—in fact, he denies them both—he at least realizes that the two are linked together. Whoever believes in freedom will believe also in the dignity of each person and will treat all people in a way that allows them to realize their own dignity in freedom. Especially in a totalitarian regime that tramples both underfoot, freedom has a special dignity.

I believe in my dignity as a person and as a Christian. At all times during World War II, I introduced myself as a Catholic priest, manifesting in this way my belief in the dignity of faith and of service to the gospel. And I came to realize that I was much less frequently vilified by insults and mistreatment than some of my fellow priests who, in order to live more peacefully, did not reveal their identity as men committed to the gospel.

During our stay in Russia, I once met a fellow priest attached to another regiment. I greeted him heartily, and by the way I greeted him, I revealed to his companions that he was a priest. I quickly realized that he was greatly embarrassed. In a low voice, so that no one else could hear him, he begged me not to disclose his identity as a priest because he already felt enough humiliated to be in Hitler's army.

I experienced my value as a person, above all, in the eucharistic celebration. There we all are united as sons and daughters of God around Christ, our Lord and our brother. On reflection, I find that during those hard years the eucharistic education I received was a special—even the central —source of strength for me, an experience of dignity and freedom.

In 1939, during my first training period, the officer in charge appointed me to serve as guard on Christmas day from midnight until late the following evening. I am sure his motive was to make me suffer by being unable to celebrate mass on Christmas. But I remained without food or drink the whole day in order to go, late that evening, to a church where I could celebrate. Today I would, of course, be free not to observe the eucharistic fast under such circumstances; yet the observance itself, under those circumstances, was a source of strength and a manifestation of inner freedom.

Because Hitler's rules so strictly forbade medical aides to celebrate the Eucharist and to preach the gospel, I could do so only at the risk of a term in jail, that is, at the risk of being deprived of free movement and activity. It would have been easy to fall into the trap of renouncing the exercise of essential freedoms in order not to be deprived even more of one's freedom. But being active as a priest throughout the war, despite the rules, strengthened this essential freedom for me, and also strengthened the inner freedom, sensitivity, and courage of many of my fellow Christians.

In June 1942 when, after being wounded, I was reappointed to a new unit, we were for about ten days in a casern in Munich. I asked for permission to celebrate or participate in the eucharistic celebration. My request was denied. So I decided to act on my own initiative. Against the rules, I left the casern late each evening, slept in our own Redemptorist house in Munich, celebrated mass very early in the morning, and returned to the casern before the soldiers were awake. All this, of course, exposed me to considerable risk, but I could dare it because I trusted that the soldiers and guards would not betray me.

By July I was back in Russia and reappointed to a new unit. I did not know what kind of treatment I would find there, but it turned out to be a happy assignment. I went immediately to the commander of the battalion with the ecclesiastical document signed by my provincial and the military bishop, which said in Latin that I had all the faculties of the Church to exercise my ministry. Of course I had no such permission according to Hitler's law. The commander understood Latin—indeed, he was a very highly cultured person—and promptly told an assistant to invite all the companies to mass on the following Sunday. "And the commander will be there too," he assured me. So my risk was rewarded. One of the officers then volunteered to serve at mass, since in his youth he had been an altar boy. So each Sunday thereafter, the men, Catholics and Protestants alike, came in great numbers to the eucharistic celebrations.

The commander and I quickly became good friends. He did not hide from me his opposition to Hitler and his party. He invited me to protect the civilians against any injustice and to call upon him in whatever circumstances I might need him.

O NE of the most rewarding ventures of freedom was my self-appointed ministry as chaplain of an SS regiment. Of course I was not officially their chaplain, but I did preach the gospel to them. It is a story worth telling.

After the long withdrawal in 1944, our unit was stationed in Poland at a new front near the Narev. A regiment of SS soldiers was among other regiments stationed there. At that time, however, many of the men recruited for the SS were not at all party members; a great number were half-German men from Czechoslovakia, Romania, the south Tyrol, and other peripheries.

When the Catholic men among them discovered that I

was a priest, they came to me often in the evenings and we shared in Bible hours and other religious talks. Then, just before Christmas, they came with the suggestion that I should say a mass for their unit on Christmas eve. I was amazed that men under the SS would dare to make such a suggestion. I knew, for instance, that only a short time before, their commander had stood before the whole unit and held up a rosary he had found in the pocket of one of the men. He threatened them with severe punishment if he found "anything like that" among them again.

So I asked, "How can you dare to take such a risk?" They answered with confident smiles, "We have blackmailed our commander! We found him and some of his fellow officers with some Polish whores, drinking the whiskey that they were to have distributed to us. So we told him that we would have a Christmas mass and he would keep his mouth shut or we would open ours!" It was after the commander's performance about the rosary that they had decided to seize this unusual opportunity to assert their own essential freedom. Needless to say, I accepted their invitation, and a great crowd of SS soldiers came to the mass on Christmas eve.

In contrast to the SS soldiers' daring was the overcautious attitude of so many Christians, exemplified at that time by the official military chaplain of the division to which we then belonged.

This chaplain telephoned our unit just before Christmas, offering to say a mass for us on the day before or the day after Christmas. The Protestant assistant to the commander thanked him for the offer but explained, "We do not need you; we have our own Catholic chaplain." The chaplain became indignant. "That is not possible!" he protested. "Well, possible or not, it is a reality," the assistant answered, and hung up the phone.

Soon after Christmas the chaplain telephoned and ordered me to see him, although he was not officially my superior. He admonished me at length about transgressing strict laws. I asked, "Whose laws? Are they God's laws or the laws of Satan?" More kindly, then, he warned me of the serious risks I was running by celebrating mass for my unit. I told him that I had said mass not only for my unit but even for an SS regiment. At that, he almost fell off his chair. Then, quite frankly, I suggested that he just drop the matter and let me do things as my conscience prompted, since it was finally my risk, not his.

I do not doubt the good intentions of the man. He probably really wanted to protect me from imprudent risks. But for me, the long dispute is unforgettable. He was a typical obedient servant of the establishment, and in the long list of my experiences, he is one of those who alerted me to the problem of irresponsible obedience and lack of courage in Christian morality.

THE risk I took in worshiping with my Polish friends led me into trouble at the beginning, and into even more serious trouble at the end, of the war. This eventually turned out to be most providential and rewarding, probably saving me from life—or death—in a Russian prison camp. However, having spoken here of rewarding experiences, I want to express my deep conviction that freedom and dignity can be preserved and increased only if we do not look for reward but seek, in the very fact that we act according to our dignity and freedom, the inner reward.

[9]

That All May Be One

THE dark years of the Third Reich, when leaders and members of the different churches were forced to suffer together and to fight together for freedom of conscience, provided strong incentives for ecumenism. They also forced us to think more about the kind of obedience we were taught toward the Church: whether it truly served maturity, growth in liberty, and commitment to liberation in the Church and the world.

I had been fairly sensitive to the Lord's wish "that all may be one," and to the need for a more positive approach to the values and charisms to be found in Protestant and Orthodox churches. However, a new kind of experience was needed to open my eyes fully to this reality.

Very early, when I was first stationed in France, a small group of Protestant friends asked me if I would conduct Bible meditations with them and for them. This I did gladly, and these evening meetings became an incentive for further sensitivity in matters of ecumenism. Again and again, then, I received encouragement from Protestant soldiers and even from Protestant officers who invited me to conduct worship for them.

Despite all the tensions and turmoil of the war years, only once did I note the slightest ungraciousness on the part of a Protestant chaplain, and that single occurrence was more amusing than annoying. It happened in Kharkov, where some of my soldier friends had prepared a huge movie theatre for religious services. An artist painted a picture of Saint George and hung it over a makeshift altar. And each Sunday I said mass in that great theatre filled with people. The Russians were amazed by the many and beautiful hymns sung by the German soldiers who participated in the mass.

The Protestant military chaplain, noting the crowds attending mass, asked in midweek for that particular hour for his service on the following Sunday. Of course he had the official right to conduct services while I, as medical helper, had none. Therefore I had to celebrate mass at the time he customarily had his service; and since there had not been enough opportunity to alert people about the change, the chaplain had the satisfaction of having a tremendous crowd that first Sunday. He then announced this time as the regular hour for his services.

But it was a disappointing experience for him. The following Sunday the chaplain had only a few people at his service while, at the hour he had reserved for my celebration of mass, the huge theatre was once more filled with worshipers, among them many Protestant Christians. Part of the reason for this was that the men did not very much like the official army chaplains: they suspected them of being all too subservient to the regime.

My direct experiences with the official Protestant chaplains were mostly friendly and pleasant. I still remember gratefully, for instance, the one who asked me spontaneously if I needed sacramental wine at the very time when I was running short of it, and generously provided me with some.

So many Protestant soldiers regularly joined me for worship, and even for the celebration of the Eucharist, that eventually I hardly knew who was Catholic and who was Protestant. Some Protestants were the most zealous and regular attendants at our common worship.

I remember one man who mentioned that he was going on leave to attend his daughter's confirmation. Only then did I discover that this soldier, who had been at my mass every Sunday and whom I considered one of our best Catholics, was a Protestant! Later, at Christmas time, I told him and other Protestant friends that their Protestant chaplain would have a prayer service at a nearby locality. He replied, "No, I have settled for our common celebration with you, so don't send me away."

More than ten years later, in Munich, I had missed a train and was looking for a car to take me on the road to my appointment. The first car that came along stopped, and the driver cried out joyfully, "Father Häring! I was at your mass every Sunday from October to Christmas in the Sumskaya Uliza in Kharkov!"

It cannot easily be expressed how much the common celebration meant for the soldiers and for me in those distressing times.

Ecumenism and the corresponding renewal of the Catholic Church was surely not possible without a new approach toward church law. Like most priests at that time, I was trained in a rather strict understanding of law and of obedience to law. The turmoil of those years had a liberating effect on me and, I am sure, on many others. Those of the younger generation who will read the following story may be amazed, but the older generation can understand it well.

A few weeks before the outbreak of the Russian war, four German priests, all as young as myself or younger, joined our company. I told them about the excellent organization we had for informing people about worship, and invited them to serve on an unofficial basis as ministers to our people. They gladly accepted. I asked if they knew about the law forbidding us, as medical aides, any religious activity, and the sanctions for disobeying the law. They said yes, they knew. I asked if they were ready to take the risks. All were ready; it meant, after all, only a few years in jail; there was no problem.

But then they raised their truly great problem, the *real* problem: they had no sacred vestments and no altar stone! Being a man of law myself, I had all these; but in this situation I promised to lend my vestments and altar stone to be divided among three of them. The fourth I assigned to celebrate mass in a church of the Uniates, where he would find all the necessary vestments and the sacred relics. The relics, however, would be not in a stone but in a linen (antimension) consecrated by a Catholic bishop of the Eastern rite.

But the poor young man clearly remembered that he was

taught, like many others, that it was a mortal sin for a priest of the Latin Church to celebrate on the antimension of the Eastern Unitate Catholics. And in spite of my eloquence, I could not convince him to the contrary. I had, however, already sent, through our clandestine organization, a message to the regiment involved that mass would be celebrated. So on Sunday morning I began harrassing my friend again, telling him, "Now you have your choice. Either you commit one 'mortal sin' on behalf of the antimension, or you commit the following dozens or hundreds of mortal sins: first, you deprive all these men of the Sunday Eucharist, and deprive a lot of them of the viaticum, the last Communion in their life; second, you will be the cause of a lot of anger and frustration among those who will come and find there is no mass; and third, you will damage trust in our secret ministerial organization which is so important in these times. So make your choice."

The man finally went, grumbling. He felt manipulated by me. But when he came back he apologized, saying that he had asked himself why he had been such a fool as to consider the altar stone more important than the celebration of the Eucharist for so many men.

Yet, even as I was speaking so forcefully to my scrupulous friends, I was having a fierce inner fight against the old legalist in myself. The dire necessity constantly to take risks in order to keep our inner freedom in an authoritarian regime helped us all to acquire gradually a healthier attitude also toward authority in our Church, and especially toward laws written under totally different circumstances.

S OON another legalistic problem came up.

When, in August of 1941, our area was under very heavy artillery fire, there was great fear for their lives among the

Russian people. I asked the mother of two young boys whether her children were baptized. She said, "Only the older one has been baptized. I brought him to a priest in Dniepropetrovsk [about a hundred miles distant], but when I took the second boy there, I could not find any priest, so he is not baptized." Perhaps no one in a free and motorized country can realize what sacrifices these two-hundred-mile journeys entailed for the parents, or the fervor of desire for their children's baptism such sacrifices represented.

The question therefore arose whether I should baptize children of Russian Orthodox parents. My memory at that time was very fresh about certain decrees of the Holy Office which forbade Catholic priests to baptize children of Orthodox Christians unless the parents would promise Catholic education. After some reflection, I realized that it would be senseless to talk about Catholic education in this area, because the Church was present only through the Orthodox Church.

In one little town where more and more people came asking for baptism, I had a long discussion with them. There were no Orthodox priests, so I asked, "Why do you Christian people not baptize your children yourselves?" But they did not consider this the ministry of lay people.

Finally, seeing that I was reluctant to baptize their children, they asked, "Have you any doubt about our orthodoxy? About the way we make the sign of the cross, for instance?" I answered that I very much liked the way they made the sign of the cross and was quite convinced that they were of the right faith. The only difficulty, I said, was that they were not in communion with the head of the Catholic Church, the bishop of Rome. They responded immediately, "But we know that Peter and Paul lived in Rome and died there, and of course we know that the bishop of Rome is the successor to Peter." I was astonished that, after so many years of Communist propaganda, they were informed even about these matters.

My reluctance to baptize their children gave way, once and forever, in the face of all the circumstances, and I rendered this service whenever I was asked, when I saw the faith of the parents and their intention to give their children a Christian education to the best of their abilities.

While we were in the Kursk district, I was receiving so many requests to baptize children that I planned to organize a great day of baptism for all, and so delayed most of the individual requests. Then, unexpectedly, our battalion was called for the second battle around Kharkov, and we had to move at a moment's notice. When this word was spread, many mothers came running to have me baptize their children, and indeed, even as I packed my little pharmacy, I performed quite a number of baptisms. Nevertheless, I deeply regretted that a considerable number of children were not yet baptized, and there was much weeping when I had to say goodbye and leave so suddenly.

In a town near Gomel where we were stationed, friendly relations with the civilians developed very easily, since they were in need of my medical help and had quickly learned that I was a priest. These people had not seen any priest in eighteen years. Very soon they were asking me to baptize their children, which I did at first on an individual basis. But then I set a special date for the baptism of all who had not been baptized, and it was one of the most wonderful liturgical experiences in my long priestly life.

The celebration took place on a Sunday afternoon. It took quite a while for them all to come together because, until the very last moment, they were trying to repair the clothes of those who were to be baptized so that they should be presentable. Yet nobody can imagine the poverty of their clothing.

All the youth were gathered, from little babies to eighteen-year-old boys and girls, young men and women. Since I had no liturgical book and did not know the Latin by heart, I celebrated this long and solemn liturgy in a spontaneous way and all in Russian. Frequently we had to interrupt the celebration because everyone was weeping, so full were their hearts.

There was even a lovely moment of humor. When the time came for me to pour the water and to "baptize in the name of the Father and of the Son and of the Holy Spirit," I began with the tallest young man. The godmother, a slight little woman, became quite nervous and finally asked her anxious question, "Father, must I take him in my arms?" Although eighteen years had passed since a baptism had been celebrated there, she still remembered that the godmother, as a sign of her responsibility, had to take the child in her arms during the baptism. We all enjoyed that moment.

I must confess that, compared with the standards of normal pastoral practice, the preparation of the parents, the godparents, and of the young people themselves for that baptism was inadequate. However, the celebration constituted a continuation of evangelization, a deepening of faith for these people—and for me as well. It was a unique experience of faith, bringing great joy to the whole population, so long deprived of pastoral care.

I came to realize the great change in my own attitude when, after being wounded in 1942, I approached the priest in the hospital in Dillingen, asking if I might celebrate mass there.

When I had been wounded, all my belongings, even my uniform and some documents, had to be thrown away because everything was covered with blood. Hence I had no means of identification. But the priest adamantly insisted that I furnish some proof of identity or else submit to an examination. I suggested that he could easily call one of our Redemptorist monasteries by phone, but he preferred the examination route. After a while, however, he gave up, seeing that in matters of theology and rubrics I was as well informed as he.

His scrupulosity did not annoy me at all, because I knew that two years before I would have acted as he did.

THESE experiences greatly helped me in the following years to honor my Church through frankness and sincerity. It would be most unfitting for me to renounce my inner freedom and the free expression of my sincere convictions within the Church after having learned to be a free man under a dictator.

[10]

Divine Providence and Human Goodness

Wʜᴇɴ I remember the war years, what comes first to my mind is praise of God's providence, and, at the same time, grateful remembrance of all those people who were, for me and for others, messengers of God's liberating goodness. Not just one, but many people—Russian, Polish, German—were actors in the daily manifestation of his providence.

Seeing the whole picture now, after so many years, I am unable to believe that all these events, and how they prepared me for the future tasks of my life, were blind coincidences. Of course, there were coincidences, but faith can readily read in them something more. In the failures and disappointments that eventually proved to be blessings, in the momentary flashes of saving inspiration, but above all in the almost unbelievable goodness of so many people, I discovered the presence of the One who cares for his children, of the divine Artist who puts pieces together and continues his work to make us masterpieces of his own goodness.

We all are meant to be instruments of this providence, coworkers and corevealers of God's fatherly love and his liberating design. It is my conviction that we all would experience more consciously his loving providence in our lives and could better convey this experience if we put all our trust in him.

Where that trust is lacking, people become niggardly; they are always looking out for themselves. But for those who trust in God's providence and generosity, the courage to give comes easily. Repeatedly I saw evidence of this in the war years, in matters both large and small.

I have already mentioned the four young priests who joined our company early in the war. In those days concelebration was not allowed; and since there was only one chalice, one altar stone, and one set of vestments, each morning before our work began we celebrated five separate masses at our beautiful altar in our barn church.

My young friends, however, had not yet learned the necessity of parsimonious use of the altar wine. In two weeks the wine I had brought with me from France, or received in small quantities from my sisters, was used up, and no mail was coming in. So I went to the Polish pastor in the next town, bringing along a very small bottle which I hoped he could fill.

The pastor received me most graciously, and when I told him of our difficulty, he immediately offered me a whole bottle of wine. I protested that I knew how hard it was for him to get wine in such times, but he answered kindly, "I have enough." When I persisted, he confessed that all he had were two bottles, of which he was offering me one. "The Lord will provide," he said.

Later in the war, almost the same thing happened again. A Polish priest asked unexpectedly if I had altar wine, and shared his last resources with me.

Small as these happenings were, for me they were signs of God's goodness shining through in the goodness of these men, and an encouragement to trust even more in his providence.

THE ways of God's providence are countless. On a certain day in Kharkov, rather early in the war, I experienced it in several of its forms.

Our army had already occupied half of the city, and I was assigned to act as interpreter on an exploratory mission with seven German soldiers. We were to go through the zones occupied by the Russian army to discover how far their soldiers had retreated.

We left on bicycles in the darkness of early morning and rode about fifteen kilometers into the area still occupied by the Russians. At one point, if we had not been warned by some Russian civilians to avoid a particular area, we would have lost our lives. Even so, we were seen by some soldiers who shot at us but did not hit any of us. The warning of the civilians was a typical reaction of those good people. It was their way of conscientious objection, of putting into practice their strong opposition to the senseless killing.

Some hours later, we were coming up a hill on our bicycles. I was in the lead; my seven tired friends were behind. At the top of the hill I was suddenly confronted by about fifty armed Russian soldiers marching toward me in perfect military formation. They were surprised, and, of course, so was I. But I was even more surprised when, on a providential impulse, I shouted like a commander, "Put up your hands!" and the Russians obeyed by throwing down their guns and raising their hands. They must have thought that there was at least a regiment behind me.

What they thought when only seven men rode up on bicycles to collect their weapons, I do not know. But when we had gathered the guns, I said to the Russians, "Go home now to your mothers, go home to your wives." And we exchanged some frank words about the nonsense of war and of killing. After that we had no fear about releasing the men. We can hope that they, too, when they have remembered that hour, have praised God's providence which so often works in unexpected ways.

It was, indeed, a day of surprises. That night, coming back from our mission, we had forgotten the name of the street from which we had started and where we would find our own unit. We remembered only that it was close to a bridge. We asked some Russian passersby for directions to "the bridge that has not been destroyed." They pointed a way, but when we came to the bridge we saw that it was not the one we sought. However, since it was already in German hands, we approached the guard. Then we heard a man cry out, "Father Häring! How does this happen? How do we meet here?" What joy it was so unexpectedly to be embraced by the brother of one of my former students and who, himself, had been with the Redemptorists for a while! He, of course, saw to it that we found our way back to our unit.

In our hardest times, when the battle of Stalingrad had come to its bitter end, divine providence manifested itself most wonderfully.

Our unit was moved, but in the moving we somehow became cut off from the rest of our army. So there we were, about three hundred soldiers, some of them wounded, and no officer with us anymore. Practically, the soldiers were relying on me, since I was the only one who knew the Russian language well. Besides, they trusted me.

Our situation was serious. We had already suffered enough under the fire of the Russian artillery, infantry, and air force; and we were in territory now held mostly by the Russians. We could surrender to them or try to find our way somehow—through how many miles of snowfields and for how many freezing days and nights?—to rejoin the German army. But we had credible information that the Russians were killing prisoners. Even if they were not, would the alternative of perhaps a lifetime in Siberia be better? On the other hand, we could be caught and shot in this territory or could die of starvation or cold on our march. We chose to march.

At my urging, the men threw away their guns. It was evident that we could not save ourselves by using force. We avoided the roads and sought our way through the fields, with those in the best health leading the way in order to trample down the snow for the weaker ones. We walked in silence.

We had agreed that we would only humbly beg people to share their daily bread with us; and I can never praise enough the compassion, mercy, and effective help we received from the good Russian people who were the angels of divine providence on this tortuous flight. They could easily have betrayed us to the Russian army, which already occupied all the long area between Voronezh and Stalingrad; but their first loyalty was to the teachings of their faith: that they could not pray to the heavenly Father for their own daily bread or for their sons to be brought home safely, unless they would share their bread with others and associate their own prayers with those of our parents and friends.

When, after many vicissitudes, we finally arrived at an evacuation hospital, and I had handed over a large number of the sick and wounded, I was made to stand trial. Who had given me the authority to lead these soldiers where I had led them? The verdict was that I was to be held there until

I could be sent to an infantry battalion known as one of the "death" battalions, composed of undesirables like me and controlled by SS officers.

I was kept in custody for a few days, so I had time to think and to meditate. One day, no food was brought to me, nor did I get any attention. I called out for food but there was no response. In the evening, I finally managed to get out of the room and, to my surprise, found that I was the only inhabitant of the huge building. Everything indicated that the German personnel had evacuated hastily, leaving behind them much materiel and, happily, their lone prisoner.

So now I had to make a choice: either to approach the Russians and give myself up, or to try again to join the German army that had treated me so unkindly. On the one hand, I feared that the Russians would suspect me of being a spy; on the other hand I feared that, emerging alone away from my unit, I might be accused of being a deserter by the German military, and sentenced to death. I trusted divine providence, and during that starlit night I found my way through the city, which was partially occupied by the Russian army, and to my great joy and that of my friends, I met the men who had been with me on the six days' walk from the Stalingrad area to Kursk.

For all of us, it was an experience like the one in the Acts of the Apostles, when Peter was freed by an angel and returned to his community. Of course, no heavenly angel had shown up, but we could not doubt God's providence. So many things had to happen, so many coincidences had to combine for this one event of liberation from distress and alienation, and for the reunion, in the vastness of the country, with just the friends who had been most grieved by our separation.

Divine Providence and Human Goodness

IN a little Polish town, Shlewitska, where we stopped for a while during our retreat from the Narev front in early 1945, God's providence allowed me to act as the messenger who brings liberation.

One morning, after I had celebrated the Eucharist in the Polish parish church, the pastor invited me to breakfast. Previously, he had been friendly and kind to me, but this was the first time he invited me to breakfast. I accepted.

Already he had told me a wonderful story of how, through divine providence, his life had been saved. Soon after the occupation of Poland by Hitler's army, he and many other Polish people were imprisoned as potentially dangerous because they would not cooperate with the injustices ordered by Hitler. Then one day, hundreds of prisoners, he among them, were being marched by the SS to be executed when, by chance, a German general, a righteous man, flew over them in his small plane and somehow realized what was happening. He landed at once and came to the rescue of the prisoners. He harshly condemned the criminals who had intended to kill them, and saw to it that the prisoners were released. The priest returned to his parish and since then had not been molested.

But that very morning, while we were still at table, two officers of the Gestapo entered and informed the pastor that he had to come with them. As motive, they cited the expectation that the town would soon be occupied by the Russians, and they wanted to protect the priest's life. Of course both the pastor and I knew quite well what "protection" meant to the Gestapo.

A providential inspiration occurred to me. With not a moment of reflection I was on my feet, playing the most farcical role of my life. I was an outraged patriot, accusing these men, with Hitler's own sharpest word, *Defätist,* of being cowards, pessimists, destroyers of people's morale. "How dare you say that the Russians will advance? You well know that our Führer has ordered that not one further inch of territory is to be yielded to the Communists, and you dare to tell the Polish people that his orders will not be fulfilled!" I asked for their identity cards and threatened to denounce them for such an insult to the Führer. Shaken, the two predators disappeared.

A little later, another Gestapo member came with the same suspicious story, to apprehend the assistant pastor. I replayed the scene with the same result. A few hours later, the Russians overran the German positions and we abandoned the village.

Ironically, the effectiveness of my performance as fanatic patriot was undoubtedly heightened by the sight of three decorations on my jacket, which I had not wanted to accept or to wear. One of them had even posed for me a question of conscience for a time, and I considered it a humiliation, since it was marked with the swastika. Yet at this particular moment they turned out to be life-saving for the two priests.

Looking back after many years, I have no feelings of guilt, as if I had lied in this game. There was no real lie involved. With such men there was no possibility of communicating truth. One could only treat them as unreal figures in a ridiculous comedy. That I could do so with no preparation and that the show had such a magical effect was, in my eyes, only possible as the work of divine providence.

AFTER the fall of Danzig, there seemed to be no escape possible. Most of the army had surrendered. But once more God's providence guided me on the path to freedom and friendships.

On a very stormy day, our battalion escaped by sea to the north. We made our way in small boats to Hela, a long peninsula stretching out about twenty miles into the Baltic Sea from the continent. Even in the cloudy and stormy weather we came repeatedly under attack by Russian war planes, but finally we landed safely on Hela's coast.

Our unit soon dug itself into the earth in a forest there, and I felt I could now continue my pastoral ministry. On Sunday, I was celebrating mass in the forest, assisted by a huge crowd of soldiers, when Captain Gerhardt, a despicable political officer, came riding on the only horse the unit had. He was an atheist and a slave of the Hitler regime.

Seeing the huge crowd celebrating with me, he burst out with curses and blasphemies, but finally decided to turn away. He could have denounced me immediately and have put me on trial for not observing the law, but he preferred to try first a diplomatic approach. He sent his assistant to tell me that if I wanted to celebrate mass or do anything of the kind, I needed his special permission. I sent back word that it was beneath the dignity of a Christian to ask an unbeliever for permission to speak on the Gospel of Matthew or that of Mark; therefore I would prefer to discontinue my ministry to the soldiers if he put me under such conditions.

But of course I did not discontinue my ministry. In a little town, Jastarnia, in the midst of the peninsula, I found that I could render some service. Indeed, some old army friends had already invited me there to celebrate mass for the soldiers. According to stringent orders in force at the time, however, I could not leave my station without a written permit. Anyone found without a permit outside of the area indicated for his own unit could be immediately executed.

My medical superior, Dr. Wegmann, who was in the neighborhood of Jastarnia, helped me in this difficulty. Whenever I wanted to go there, he sent me an order to come to report to him. So, not only on Sundays but even on weekdays, I celebrated the liturgy and preached the Good News for the soldiers there and, behind locked doors, for the Polish population as well.

Captain Gerhardt did finally denounce me and organized a trial against me, not so much for having said mass as for having manifested an antiwar and anti-Hitler attitude. Especially in those last desperate days of the war, this meant extreme danger. But when I came out from the second hearing, a huge crowd of soldiers was there shouting threatening words at the captain. "If we become prisoners, our last bullet will be for you!" they promised. Gerhardt was frightened enough to suspend, for the time being at least, the trial against me.

A few days later, when he was still intending to pursue the case against me, he stepped on a mine. The explosion destroyed one of his legs and badly wounded the other. I was nearby and gave him the best care I could, and later brought him to a boat (an evacuation hospital) in Hela's harbor. Thus he was one of the last men to escape to the west.

Some years after the war, when he learned my address from other men of our unit who had returned from war prisons, this man wrote me a friendly letter of gratitude. I returned greetings and said no word about the troubles he had caused me. He is a poor cripple who has suffered and been punished enough for his own foolishness. Besides, as things turned out, I could hardly harbor ill feelings against him, since I realized later that divine providence had made of his harsh action a coincidental instrument of liberation for me.

WHEN I realized that the time had come when our army would surrender, I got in touch with some German-speaking Catholic fishermen of Jastarnia, who attended my masses there. They owned two huge fishing boats, and I knew that to save their own lives they would want to leave the area before the Russians came, and seek a new home in Western Germany.

On a stormy day, I rowed out to them in a small boat to ask if they could take about two hundred of my companions and try to escape during the night. It would be too risky, of course, to put the two hundred men on the boats at that spot, but they arranged a certain point where the boats could dock during the night.

As it would be impossible to complete this move without at least the passive tolerance of the commander, I approached him and told him about the opportunity, in which he could share if he wished. While this man had not been very sympathetic toward me, he had been tolerant and respectful. I told him quite frankly that, in our minds, the war had come to an end and it was meaningless for us to wait passively until the Russians would capture us. He thanked me for the offer and was inclined to allow the action, but his assistant, the same Captain Wöhrle who had been responsible for the cow-stealing episodes and for the killing of several people in the Pripet swamps, violently opposed the idea, saying that my suggestion was a coward's way out. This same man, however, along with the commanding general, took the last big boat that left the harbor, and escaped.

Unable now to put into practice what had been so well planned, I had to inform my friends on the fishing boats, who would be waiting during the night. I therefore sent three of my best young friends to meet them in the dark and to leave with them. These three later became captives of the British but very soon after the war were released and returned to their families. I, too, could have escaped with them, but as a priest I would have set a bad example by saving my own life without saving as many of my friends as possible. Moreover, I would have missed the unique experience of the goodness and courage of my Polish friends in Jastarnia, through whom divine providence would so wonderfully manifest itself.

THE conflict with Captain Gerhardt, the political officer whose intolerance had prevented my celebrating the Eucharist in the forest when we first came to Hela, was one of the most providential events in my life. I could not then foresee what it would mean for my future when I went for the first time to celebrate mass in the parish church and thus met the generous Polish people who, trusting in God's gracious help, became the effective and active instruments of his providence.

Very soon I made some very good friends there, including especially the church sacristan, Alphons Konke, and his father, who had been mayor of the town when it belonged to Poland. The Konke family spoke both Polish and German but were wholly Polish in their thinking and in their culture. For them I was a priest and a brother in Christ.

When our army surrendered, practically the whole peninsula of Hela became a huge Russian prison camp. All of us in that area who belonged to the German military were consequently sealed in as war prisoners in a seemingly hopeless situation.

Early one day, Alphons Konke came to my quarters with a few friends. They gave me a package and told me to change my clothes. In the package was clerical clothing, and their scheme was that I should now become their Polish pastor and thereby escape identity as a prisoner.

For several reasons I was, at first, quite reluctant to follow their orders. In the first place, I had qualms of conscience about separating from my soldier friends who, in this terrible situation, needed my presence, both as priest and medic. Secondly, I considered it an all too risky affair for these Polish friends. Besides, although the plan might allow me to avoid being transported, possibly to Siberia, it also risked my being discovered by the Russians and being shot as an escaped prisoner.

Finally the men agreed with me that I should talk the matter over with my best friends in the army, to see how they would feel if I remained behind while they had to expect to be taken off to inner Russia. I did talk it over with those soldier friends who were the most faithful members of the Church, and they were very realistic in their assessment of the situation. They felt, as I did, that it would be a great loss to be separated, but they said we could scarcely hope that the Russians would allow us to stay together in any event, and that I should take this chance that was offered me. So the moment came when I threw away the uniform of a German medical aide and dressed as a priest.

Alphons Konke offered me a room in his house, and there I could feel at home. He had a beautiful family life with a good wife and seven children. His father and mother lived in an apartment in the same house. His father became like a father to me, and was one of my chief advisers.

Whatever this wise man told me to do, I could safely do. And his suggestion was that I immediately take up my new appointment as their pastor: pastor by grace of the people. Their real pastor had earlier been marked by the Gestapo for deportation and had gone into hiding outside of his parish. They hoped that he would return—and indeed he did return later, but as a sick man.

The very next day I celebrated the Eucharist for the local people, and on the following Sunday I read the gospel in Polish and made the announcements as grandfather Konke had written them down for me. Everyone in the church was nervous except me. Through my experiences in the war, my nerves had become hardened; but I think it was also a special grace of trust in God.

One memory of this time, however, lingers regretfully in my mind. A few days after my appointment as pastor, a Protestant chaplain of the German army, accompanied by a few soldiers, came to see me at the Konke house. He explained that his soldiers would very much like to have a religious service before being deported to inner Russia, and asked permission to celebrate worship in our church. For me, this request was most embarrassing. Not for anything in the world would I want to hurt the feelings of this good chaplain or his Protestant soldiers; but on the other hand, it was unthinkable that my Polish friends would approve of offering him the use of the church for a Protestant service. So I decided to tell him the plain truth: that only a few days before, I had been a prisoner myself and was pastor only by adoption. He understood immediately and made no further request.

Since the whole peninsula was a well-guarded prison, the Russians tolerated some movement among the prisoners. Thus I was able to receive some visits from men of my unit who wanted to say goodbye. Later, with a heavy heart, I saw them again when they were a part of that long pitiful procession that started away toward inner Russia. What could I do now but pray for them and continue to pray for them, that a benign providence would protect them and help them to discover the meaning of their terrible experience?

Not long after I settled in the sacristan's house, the Russian commander of the town decided to live there too, since the house was clean and had several good rooms.

The morning he was to come, I told my friends that I was terribly ill with a high fever, and had to go to bed. Although my skin had been darkened by so much exposure, I really looked that day as ashen as a man who had been sick a long time. The commander came an hour or two later, looking through all the rooms which he thought he might occupy. He also came into my room where I was lying as a sick man in bed. He showed some concern, and since it was shortly after the day when the German army had finally surrendered and the war was ended, he said in a friendly tone, "It is not a good time to be sick just when the war is over. But we have freed you now, and I hope you will soon be out of your sickroom." As a sign of friendship, then, he offered me a big cigar.

When the commander had chosen his rooms, limiting us quite sharply, Grandfather Konke came to see me. I had intended to ask him where I would hide now, but he was jubilant. "Father, this is marvellous! In the lion's den you will be safe." He had given me the right solution before I could ask the question. And indeed, the presence of the Russian commander was the most effective life insurance for me. Who would suspect that a German medical aide would hide in the very house in which the Russian commander had his headquarters?

Although living in the same house with the town's Russian commander insured my safety, it was not always equally agreeable to live side by side with some other Russian officers.

Very soon one young officer moved in who caused considerable trouble. He went around to the neighbors, and even to Alphons Konke himself, requesting their wives for the night. Because of him, people lived in constant anguish. One evening he took a girl from the neighborhood into his room. Happily, in his drunkenness the night before, he had destroyed the electric light; so while he was trying to make light, the girl was able to escape by jumping through the window to the ground, about ten feet below.

The men of the parish came in groups to ask me what to do on similar occasions, and even asked frankly if they could have a general absolution to do away with such a monster and bury him somewhere deep in a cellar. These, of course, were anguishing thoughts.

On the other hand, there were some quite admirable Russian officers. Alphons Konke had horses, and every second Sunday he drove me to the village of Kusnizka, about five miles distant, where there was no pastor and I was expected to celebrate mass. The Russian commander of that village asked one Sunday if he could have a place in our wagon, and as we drove, we talked together.

He showed himself to be a well-educated, gentle person who was also respectful of religious convictions. From then on, he allowed his soldiers to absent themselves from army service during my Sunday mass, and a good number of them did come to mass regularly. Since I never could be sure that all those who came to mass did not have a spy among them, I learned my sermon by heart each week, so that nobody could detect the fact that I was not a Polish priest.

THE first time I had to face Stalin-worship as a reality in occupied Poland was rather embarrassing.

I was standing outside the house one day with my friend Alphons Konke and the organist-cantor, when one of the Russian officers who had a room in the Konke house called all three of us for what he called a "friendly dialogue." Immediately he started unveiling a picture of Stalin, extolling and praising him. We remained mute as we listened, and he became more and more impatient with us. Finally I realized that we had to make some gesture of person-worship to the honor of Stalin; and I remember how happy I was when I thought of an ambiguous word and could say, "He is a very stout and strong fellow." The Russian word for "stout" is *tolstoy,* and can have a more or less noble meaning.

The officer seemed content with that, and Alphons Konke found a similar phrase. However, the organist, after searching desperately for a word that would rescue him, could only say, "This man has liberated us." The next day the organist asked me whether he must go to confession before receiving communion, because he felt guilty about having called Stalin a "liberator."

ONLY a few days later, in one of the strange ways in which God's providence guided me, Stalin served as a kind of liberator for me through an order he gave, just at the proper time, regarding treatment of Polish priests by the army.

Grandmother Konke had rushed in from the street to warn me, "Father, go quickly into the next room and hide under the bed. The Russian soldiers are gathering all men today and taking everyone's identity card so that no one can escape from work."

I started to take the advice, but before I could disappear under the bed, the Russian soldiers stood in the main room, and there was nothing to do but to greet them quietly. As expected, their first word was, "Hand over your identity card; you have to go to work." But I did not yet have—as I would a few days later—a Polish identity card, so the embarrassment could have been very serious. So I answered quite sternly, "Don't you know that I am the pastor of this place? I don't go to work." And then I asked another question which surprised even myself. "Don't you know that Marshal Stalin has given strict orders to respect the Polish priests?" It was a question, not a statement, but they took it as an infallible word and immediately apologized and disappeared. On two other occasions I was able to rescue myself from embarrassing situations by asking the same question with the same success.

Nevertheless, I continued to be uneasy about this ruse. Then in 1954, at an international congress of moral theologians in Luxemburg, I was having an afternoon walk with a colleague, Professor Heribert Doms, who had been a professor in Breslau and later in Münster. He told me that when the Russians occupied Breslau, he and many priests were imprisoned and not treated well; but suddenly, around the middle of May, they were set free, given abundant and good clothing, and told that this was the order of Marshal Stalin.

I do not dream that Stalin acted out of love for our priestly vocation. However, his political decision turned out to be a real liberation for me. Divine providence had led me to ask the right question.

[11]

My Polish Brothers and Sisters

I have been recounting the blessings of divine providence in order to share with the reader my gratitude to the chief agents of these providential happenings, my Polish friends.

As in Russia, so in Poland, particularly in Jastarnia and Kusintzka, I often experienced the faith and Christian love that transcends all the ethnic divisions and the hatreds sown by nationalism, materialism, and lust for power.

Like all of us, my Polish friends had their human limitations and weaknesses; but even these contributed toward the whole picture of a wonderful humanity of warmth, goodness, gentleness, and mutual trust. I could write at length about all the members of the great Konke family and their friends who also became my friends: about Martha, the busy, slightly old-fashioned but courageous and faithful housekeeper for Father Stefansky, the real pastor; about Ambrose, my friendly neighbor; about Mr. Shebrowsky, the president of the local soviet; and last but not least, about Father Stefansky himself.

L ET us begin with Martha's resolution of a very chancy situation.

When Father Stefansky came back to the parish, I moved from the Konke house to the rectory. One morning Martha called me from my room to tell me that the Communist mayor and two Russian officers wanted to speak with me, since Father Stefansky was ill. I saw that Martha was quite interested in what they might want to talk about, for she threw me a meaningful glance before disappearing hurriedly into the kitchen.

And what did they want to talk about? They told me that our parishoners were hiding a lot of things, possibly including weapons, under the roof of the church. I did know that they were hiding some grain and some clothes there, because nothing was safe from robbery or confiscation. Now I realized that Martha had gone to mobilize the people to carry everything away, so it was up to me to entertain my guests for a while.

We still had some good whiskey left for such occasions. I also had some cigarettes, so I invited them to stay because I had an important matter to discuss with them. I told them that in the last days of the war, the Germans had removed the roof from the church in the village of Kusnizka, and it was now exposed to the rains because I could not find anything with which to replace it. Did they think that I could have some roofing from barracks left by the Germans, and if so, how should I make the request, and to whom? They gave detailed instructions, and together we began to calculate the material we would need, how we would transport it, and so on. Indeed, we got into such an interesting conference that they seemed to have forgotten the main business for which they had come.

When I thought there had been enough time for the people to have removed everything under our church roof, I reminded them of their errand. We went over and, as I had hoped, we found the great space under the roof empty and clean. Martha's warning system had worked perfectly. My visitors were angry, not at me but at those who, they thought, had made false accusations. I even had to plead with them not to take any further steps because whoever had spoken of these matters had probably done so in good faith.

M ARTHA'S loyalty was total, but on another occasion it was a bit perverse.

Before the pastor had gone away, he had owned two cows which later disappeared. Martha was convinced that one of these had survived and was being kept by a family in the parish. Then one day, the cow showed up in the stall in the pastor's barn, and Martha's version was that the cow had spontaneously sought and found her real owner. The pastor and I were not at all convinced of this, and were in agreement that the cow must be brought back to the family, where its milk was needed for the children. But Martha considered that we were thus cooperating with injustice. And later, when the pastor and I even went to visit the family as a sign of friendship, Martha punished—and amused—us by not preparing dinner.

However, soon after, Father Stefansky was confined to bed with fever, and Martha did everything in her power to atone for that one small lapse.

O NE of my friendliest neighbors was Ambrose, an open-hearted, hard-working fisherman, one of those most concerned that the priests should have, each day, a good ration of fresh fish.

During the first months, Ambrose was sober and abstinent, since whatever alcoholic beverage had been available was put aside for "resolving" any troublesome cases that might come up with the Russian military: if, for instance, they should discover that I was an escaped prisoner of war. But when the fishermen's economic situation improved, Ambrose returned to his bottled source of consolation and merriment.

When we met on one of his very merry days, our dialogue became somewhat confused; so I said to him, "Ambrose, if only you would not drink so much, you would surely be our finest parishioner." With a bow, and in the tone of a great gentleman, he immediately retorted, "And you, Father, whether I am drunk or not, are surely our finest pastor!" So how could I then talk further of reform?

On another day Ambrose told me the story of an unsuccessful attempt at reform. At the end of a parish retreat preached by Jesuit priests, he was persuaded, along with other hard drinkers, to make a public appearance and to swear before the whole parish that he would give up drinking. He really meant it, he said, and kept his oath for quite a while. But then something changed the situation.

At the end of the season, the fishermen divided the profits, keeping a certain amount for a social gathering where everyone enjoyed his whiskey. Ambrose felt that he had certainly not made a vow of abstinence in order that others could drink his share as well as their own, so he decided that, for this one occasion, he was free to join his friends. The next morning, however, he decided that since he had broken his solemn promise, he was no longer bound by it.

That was the way Ambrose explained the story to me. I

was not as convinced about his casuistry as he would have wished.

ONE of my best friends in Jastarnia, Mr. Shebrowsky, was the elected president of the local soviet, and in that position he felt a special obligation to help me with his good advice in any difficult situation. Each Sunday evening he visited me. Being a highly educated and much traveled man, and above all, graced with a good sense of humor, he was always a pleasant visitor. But, on one occasion a problem arose which he could not immediately resolve.

He had heard that the officer of the political police (NKVD), Jusip by name, while drinking with other men, had expressed serious misgivings about "the new pastor" because, he said, I favored my two German altar boys. This surprised me because I did not even know that the boys were German. They always spoke to me in Polish, or rather in their dialect; but Jusip knew that one boy had a German great-grandfather and the other a German great-grandmother. Possibly, too, the families may have used the German language during the German occupation. At any rate, now they were being labeled as Germans.

I told Mr. Shebrowsky that I could not tell the boys that just because of a little bit of German blood they should not show up so frequently, especially since they knew quite well about my own German blood. Just then, Mr. Shebrowsky chuckled as if a bright idea had struck him, and said, "Never mind, we'll find a solution; I shall tell you next Sunday."

But I did not have to wait until Sunday. The very next morning, when I was upstairs in the rectory after saying mass, I heard loud voices from the street below. Looking down, I saw my friend Shebrowsky and officer Jusip staggering in our direction, so inebriated that they needed the whole width of the street for their meanderings. I had only one hope, that they would not come into the rectory; but in a few moments, Martha called me, and there they were.

Mr. Shebrowsky, in a most imperial tone, gave orders to Jusip to kneel down and to swear that he would never again say anything against the new pastor. Jusip, however, answered that he had a more important position and therefore would not take orders from one who was only the president of the local soviet. But the president was considerably smarter, and he convinced Jusip that he was the one to give orders. So Jusip swore a false oath that he had never said anything against me; but he added a serious oath that he would always protect the local priest. Then off they went.

The following Sunday, Mr. Shebrowsky came to visit as usual, greeting me with "Praised be Jesus Christ," the way people customarily greeted each other there. Then he had a strange question. He said he remembered that on Monday morning he had met Jusip and had invited him to have a drink in order to settle the matter about the altar boys, but he didn't remember what had happened then. Had he, perhaps, tried to see me? I told him then, to our mutual amusement, how splendid his performance had been on Monday morning.

WHEN the old pastor, Father Stefansky, returned to the parish, we lived together in the rectory. I could not imagine a better friend than this cordial, gentle, and trusting man. In the beginning, I repeatedly asked his advice about how to do things. Then one day he said: "I am a man of the old school, and you are a young man of a new school. Why, then, do we not just do things as each of us thinks right? You need not ask me." But I did make clear to him that I considered it always good for a younger man to learn from the wisdom of the older ones. Besides, not being of Polish origin, I needed the advice of a man who knew the people more intimately.

For several weeks Father Stefansky was very ill. He had a high fever, yet he would say his whole breviary daily and, of course, it would take him some hours. I tried to persuade him that he was not obliged to do this when he was sick. But with a beautiful smile he told me, "You are really right but you do not know the ways of human weakness. If I once started excusing myself, I don't know where I would stop."

THE pastor, as well as the people who had arranged the mode of my escape from the prison camp, had hoped that I would stay with them in Jastarnia. But in September I began to speak of my intention to return to Germany. I first revealed this intention when an unusual visitor came to the rectory.

Father Stefansky had been invited to a Russian-Polish celebration of peace and reconciliation in Hela, the peninsula's chief settlement, which was a part of our parish. A Russian admiral had accompanied him home, and we were able to have a good exchange of experiences and opinions in the rectory. This high-ranking man, decorated with the Lenin order, expressed his respect for religious faith, and I felt that he was sincere. We spoke of our many parishioners who were in Denmark and Eastern Germany, and I asked if there might be a possibility to contact them. The admiral told us that the issuance of permits for such travel had just been given over to the Polish authority.

When our visitor had left, Father Stefansky asked if I was actually thinking about visiting the absent parishioners or if I was perhaps thinking about something else. I told him frankly that I had a great desire to return to Germany because my parents would be celebrating their golden jubilee in a few weeks and they did not even know if I was still alive; there had been no way to send them a message.

Father Stefansky understood this motive and set out to find a remedy. A few days later he told me that a German officer who had saved a number of Polish people's lives had been hidden in one of the houses of the parish, and secret arrangements were now being made to allow him to return to Germany. "So now he can carry a message to your parents," the priest said. (And indeed, I found out later, when I reached home, that the message did get through. The officer arrived almost at the same hour as I did.)

I still felt, however, that the time had come for me to return to Germany. When the people heard this, many tried to dissuade me, and Father Stefansky told me bluntly that, while he understood my desire and would not oppose it, I should not expect him to help bring about the loss it would mean if I left. But when everyone understood that I really wanted to leave, my friend Shebrowsky and Grandfather Konke made arrangements to procure the necessary papers. They managed to get an official permit for travel to Berlin and, in addition, a strong recommendation, written in both Polish and Russian, from the governor of the province. And to my great surprise, they brought also a letter of recommendation from Jusip, the local head of the political police.

So at last I said goodbye to the many dear friends in Jastarnia; and there were tears on both sides.

TWENTY-SEVEN years later, in 1972, I was invited by the Catholic Academy of Warsaw and the Catholic University of Lublin to give a few lectures. There was also an inspiring meeting with Polish professors of moral theology, some of whom had been my students in Rome.

On that occasion, without any previous notice, I visited Jastarnia, accompanied by the superior of the Polish Redemptorists and one of the moral theologians. I went first to Alfons Konke's house. His wife and children recognized me immediately, but I had to learn the sad news that Alphons and quite a number of my other friends had died. The cordiality of the welcome by so many friends amazed my two Polish confreres. As for me, I was so overwhelmed, so filled with gratitude toward these good people, that I could not sleep the next two nights.

There was only one little disappointment: I needed frequent help from one of my confreres as interpreter, and my Jastarnia friends could not believe it. "How could you forget the Polish language?" But not one little thing that had happened during my stay there in 1945 was forgotten. We recalled them all with joy. Meanwhile, the people had heard about my activity during the Second Vatican Council; and when they spoke of it, I could remind them that they themselves had been the instruments of God's providence which allowed me to assist in that work.

All the details of my travel back to Germany in the fall of 1945 had to be retold. My friends wanted to know how well the Lord had heard their prayers for me, since during the ten days following my departure, fervent prayers were offered at each hour of the day and night for my safe journey. Each family took its turn during one hour. They called it "the living rosary"; and their joy was great when they heard how God's gracious providence had guided and protected me during my journey home.

[12]

The Way Home

In October of 1945 I left Jastarnia. And sad though I was to leave the wonderful friends there, my heart soared when the train pulled out from Gdynia for Stettin, the first stop on the way home to my own country, my own family, my Redemptorist community, and to a full-time ministry as priest, unimpeded by the conditions of war.

Despite their poverty, the good people of Jastarnia had provided me with a few new shirts and, even more important, with bread and a generous supply of smoked fish. When the fishermen heard that I was about to leave, they began, earlier than usual, the work of smoking the best fish so that they could be sure I would not starve on the long journey.

In Stettin I immediately looked for the nearest rectory and, by chance, found there a German pastor. Before the war the town had been wholly German, but now it was on the borderline between Poland and Eastern Germany, and its population was predominantly Polish. This one German priest had remained to care for the German Catholics. He welcomed me cordially, and I stayed the night with him. I

111

saw that he was almost starving to death, and so decided to leave him half of my bread and smoked fish. My first impulse had been to give him all of the fish, but then, calculating how many days I would be traveling and how much I would need, I finally yielded to self-concern and kept half for myself.

In the train from Stettin to Berlin, I sat beside a Polish priest who, for the first time in his life, was going to visit Berlin. But before we crossed the border, a group of Russian soldiers came into the train and robbed us of all we had. I lost the new shirts, the bread, and the good smoked fish; and I blamed myself for not having left all the food with the starving priest in Stettin. All that was left to me was my prayerbook, the breviary. When the Russian soldier began to take that, I asked him if he wanted to use it for his prayers. He was so angered by the question that he flung the book at my head. So I had at least this one companion for the rest of my journey.

My first task in Berlin was to find the vicar general of the diocese, since the pastor in Stettin had asked me to bring a message to his bishop, and had given me the address. When I asked the first person I met how to find this address, the gentleman told me that there were ruins all around and he was sure I could not find it by myself. "So, if you will allow me," he said, "I will accompany you." It took more than an hour of my guide's time, and he did not leave me until I had found the vicar general. As a southern German I had always been a bit prejudiced against "Prussians." This experience changed my feelings radically.

The vicar general took my message, shared his poor meal generously with me, and then brought me to the Redemptorist monastery in Berlin where, of course, I got a fine welcome.

Now I had to face a reality that I had refused to worry

about until now. That was the fact that my permits were valid only from Jastarnia to Berlin and then back from Berlin to Poland. My friends in Poland had figured that the only way to obtain a permit at all was to get one from Jastarnia to Berlin and back again. It would then be up to my confreres in Berlin to find some way for me to proceed from there.

My confreres went to the commander of the British section of Berlin to get a permit to travel to the borderline between East and West Germany. As our Redemptorists have a monastery in Heiligenstadt, in the Eichsfeld, just at the border into West Germany, I was soon on my way and was cordially received at the monastery. My Eichsfeld confreres then tried to discover if there might be some way through fields or woods to cross the borderline during the night. The result was absolutely negative. The Russians had just organized the most severe control. The entire border was lit up during the night and guarded so closely that my confreres were convinced that it would be a most unreasonable risk to try to cross at any point.

However, since I had hurried my departure from Poland in order to be home on the day of my parents' golden jubilee, and since I had unlimited trust in God's providence, I decided to try to walk through the control stations.

There were three stations. The first control man, seeing me in priest's clothes, did not even ask a question; he simply let me walk through. I passed the second Russian station hidden in a load of hay in a farmer's cart. Then I prepared myself to cross the last and most official station. I knew that nobody was allowed to pass this last station without the proper permits, and mine, although written in both Polish and Russian, were surely not proper.

To my surprise, one of the two soldiers at the military control post was slumped over, snoring in a drunken stupor.

I greeted the other and handed him the letter of recommendation that had been given me in Jastarnia, hoping that he would not read it too carefully. I saw that he read the Polish text first, so knew that this was his mother tongue. Then he addressed me in good Polish saying, "Father, I am sorry but this permit does not authorize you to pass this border point and, as you know, we soldiers might risk five to ten years in jail if we let you pass."

At the time there were a few people around, and I realized that the risk would be too great under the circumstances. So I conversed with him a while, asking how he came to the Russian army. He told me that the earlier division of Poland, agreed upon by Stalin and Hitler, had brought him into long military service in the Russian army. He was a Catholic, and it was obvious that he had reverence for a priest.

When, a little later, the coast was clear and nobody could observe us, I said to him suddenly, "Thank you for letting me go," and ran past. Now I was in no-man's-land, singing loudly in German the most solemn hymn of praise and thanksgiving.

The spot where I had crossed the border was the triangle where the Russian, American, and British forces of occupation met. So now I presented myself at the American post of control. The only soldier there was entertaining himself with a girl. He looked at my papers and reacted with only a sharp backward motion of his hand, and one word, "Back! Back! Back!" I could not believe it. I stood looking at him in amazement. In a few moments he became furious and, loading his gun, shot over my head. So I knew that he was terribly serious.

I went, then, to the British control. Three soldiers there were examining a number of women with their children, who evidently did not have the necessary permits. When my turn came, one of the soldiers greeted me in a friendly way and asked if I were a Jesuit. When I said, "No, I am a Redemptorist," he embraced me cordially, saying that he lived next door to a Redemptorist monastery and had many friends there. He offered me a cigarette and asked no questions whatever about my papers.

It was here that I heard the probable explanation of my previous good luck at the Russian control station. The women who came with their children had bribed a Russian officer, by giving him several bottles of whiskey, to make the one difficult watchman drunk and to persuade the other one to let them pass when nobody was watching. As the one to be persuaded was the Polish man who had allowed me to go through, I feel that his own officer's persuasion to allow the women to go through might have given him the courage to let me pass too. At any rate, I praised the Lord who, so surprisingly, had arranged a unique situation for my passage from the Soviet paradise into the free world.

After walking several miles to Göttingen, I again experienced the goodness of people. A man approached me and said, "Father, you look exhausted; you must be hungry. Will you come and share some bread and butter with me?" Having spent the whole day on my feet and without food, I was most grateful for his offer. He was evidently a rather poor man, but he shared his modest ration with me.

Then finally, I was on the train that would cross the border between the British and the American occupation zones. The control there was very thorough. As a result, I, along with dozens of other people who, like me, had no permits, was ordered off the train and told to take the next train back to Göttingen.

We waited there half the night. But when the next train came, going toward the American zone, I saw a young American soldier helping a mother with small children. He listened to her kindly and then went to an American officer and got permission for her to travel on. So I, too, went to this young man who had a feeling heart, and explained a part of my story. Immediately he ran to the same officer, and this kindly officer put me on the train. So controls were behind me.

Perhaps it was best that I first had to experience the depersonalizing behavior of bureaucracy so that I could appreciate the more the wonderful goodness of some who, in their sensitivity to the needs of others and their desire to help them, were true instruments of God's providence.

Several days later, when I arrived at my home town, I first met one of my sisters. Her joyous outcry was, "What a joy this is for our father!" For our father *only?* So I knew that there would be no jubilee celebration. My sister had found the best way to express the message that our mother had gone to her eternal rest some time before.

It was a cold and stormy October day when I came home. One of the first things I learned was that father had no clothes for me to change into. Toward the end of the war, he had given away his own clothes and mine to German soldiers, so that, by wearing civilian clothes, they might avoid prison camp. That was one of the best pieces of news I could receive.

When evening came, my father was getting ready to go to church to the October rosary service. Since the night was so stormy, I suggested that although I would go, he could stay at home. His response was, "At the beginning of this month I made it my intention not to miss for a single day the mass and the rosary, and that I would pray for your homecoming. What a shame if now I would not go to give thanks!"

Thanks be to God!